THE UNIVERSAL LEADERSHIP MODEL

THE UNIVERSAL LEADERSHIP MODEL

Simplicity on the Other Side of Complexity

by Brett Thomas

First Print Edition, November 2023

Copyright © 2023-2025 Brett Thomas and Integral Publishing, LLC

No part of this publication may be reproduced, stored in a retrieval system, or transmitted in any form or by any means, electronic, mechanical, photocopying, recording, or otherwise, without written permission of the publisher.

ISBN 9798339007029

Published by Integral Publishing, LLC

Printed in the U.S.A.

First printing November 2023

CONTENTS

INTRODUCTION 1

CHAPTER 1: BOGUS LEADERSHIP 5

CHAPTER 2: LEADERSHIP THEORY PRIMER 25

CHAPTER 3: THE LEADERSHIP ROSETTA STONE 67

CHAPTER 4: LEADERSHIP ABILITIES AND COMPETENCIES 77

CHAPTER 5: BUILDING A UNIVERSAL MODEL OF LEADERSHIP 91

CHAPTER 6: USING THE RIGHT STYLE WITH THE RIGHT FOLLOWERS 109

CHAPTER 7: EVALUATING LEADERSHIP ABILITY 155

CHAPTER 8: LEADERSHIP PRACTICES 189

CONCLUSION 197

INTRODUCTION

This short book introduces you to a true breakthrough in the field of leadership and leadership development: The Universal Leadership model. In a field where most so-called "experts" cannot agree on a single definition of effective leadership, and certainly none of their leadership frameworks offer any consistency or coherency, having a "model" of leadership that works universally, across all contexts and cultures is a welcome addition to the field.

It is not lost on me that there are as many "models" of leadership as there are leadership advice givers. I am well aware that it is a very big claim to say that this model is "universal." This is a claim I will back up over the course of the coming pages and the short chapters in this short, quick-read book.

You are familiar with the phrase, "Beauty is in the eye of the beholder." In the same way, as I put it, "Leadership is in the eye of the follower."

As you will learn in this book, it is the follower's values, beliefs, worldviews, needs and preferences that determine what "effective leadership" will be for <u>them</u>.

However, many (if not most) leadership training programs and leadership frameworks emphasize the personality traits (or qualities as they call them) of the leaders and underemphasize or even completely ignore followers! This, of course, is completely ridiculous, but it is a fact. So, any leadership model or framework that leaves out followers is flawed from the start (which rules out many of them)

Also, many leadership frameworks ignore the context in which leadership occurs.

The context, or as I often call it the "circumstances", plays a crucial role in determining what kind of leadership approaches will be useful, helpful, and embraced by the people in those circumstances (as opposed to being resisted or rejected altogether).

Again, many, if not most, leadership models ignore the context (the circumstances) and simply recommend a one-size-fits-all approach. That is if they even recommend an approach, since many emphasize leader character traits (qualities) and don't even describe approaches (techniques, behaviors or specific practices).

As we will explore together, many leadership advice-givers have many ideas about what leadership is and how it works. However, when you start to dig into the books and trainings that purport to help people get better at leadership, you can get bogged down very quickly.

Most leadership trainings and many books about leadership fail to define the specific abilities, skill sets, skills, techniques and behaviors of leadership.

When they leave this essential information out, it makes it very difficult for leaders to actually improve their leadership skills.

This book, and the Universal Leadership Model that it describes, is a remedy for that.

This book is based on over 20 years of experience advising leaders, training leaders, and coaching leaders and executive teams. My experience avails me a unique perspective on what methods actually produce improvements in leadership skills versus which methods only increase a leader's knowledge of concepts but do little to nothing to change his or her behavior.

I am approaching this book as a conversation with you, the reader.

I am assuming that you are already familiar with many aspects of leadership (and leadership development); otherwise, you would not have been interested enough (by the title) to even pick up this book.

I have authored many books detailing the specific dimensions and use of this model, but for this introduction, I have kept this book short. This way, you can easily get through the whole book and have a high-level understanding of this model in just a few hours. If you find this model intriguing and/or valuable, I hope that we can "continue this conversation" in one of my many other books.

My other books on leadership development all refer back to the Universal Leadership Model, but they go into a lot more detail applying the leadership practices (including numerous specific techniques and behaviors) as well as focusing on increasing leaders' versatility using the different leadership styles.

Before we can have a serious conversation about a universal leadership model, or any serious leadership framework for that matter, we must first have a serious conversation about the "elephant in the room."

The elephant in the room is the well-understood fact that most leadership development efforts fail, and according to many analysts, the leadership development industry as a whole has failed. Let's address the very serious issue of bogus leadership in Chapter 1.

CHAPTER 1:
BOGUS LEADERSHIP

Many studies from best-in-class organizations, institutions and publications in recent years have drawn the same conclusion: most leadership development efforts fail. This is no exaggeration, this is simply a matter of fact that is easily verified. Numerous studies from prominent institutions (including McKinsey and Harvard) estimate that approximately 80 cents of every dollar spent on leadership development is wasted. I have personally reviewed numerous studies that back up this assertion.

This also tracks closely with my two decades of experience training and coaching leaders, and also reviewing leadership development programs and interviewing facilitators and participants who have gone through typical leadership development programs.

I have devoted my professional career to this field of leadership development and it has been of great interest to me to stay on top of the current industry practices and compare my unique methodology to what my peers and competitors are doing. I am very familiar with how leadership training and coaching is typically done (and how it is very slowly evolving).

Most leadership training programs amount to one and two-week classroom seminars with lectures about leadership character traits, leader qualities, or abstract concepts that have little bearing on learning the actual concrete techniques (behaviors) that can improve leadership performance.

I'm sure you have come into contact with this problem. When you try to read books, attend leadership seminars or speak to executive coaches, it seems that they all have a different idea of what constitutes effective leadership, and they largely contradict each other.

Bernard Bass, the well-respected leadership researcher and author of *The Bass Handbook of Leadership: Theory and Managerial Applications,* has noted, "Any two-day conference on leadership begins with one day of argumentation about what leadership means."

Many business professors, when speaking candidly, admit this fact that no one can agree on a definition or description of effective leadership. MIT Sloan management professor John Van Maanen has stated, "Even today, three-plus decades in, there's no real definition of it."

William Deresiewicz, the author of the book, *Excellent Sheep*, points out while every college in the country claims to be producing leaders, no one appears to know what the word even means. "There seem to be two possibilities," he writes, "The first is that it means nothing at all, or whatever definition is useful at any given time. The second is that it simply means being in charge."

Another well-known theorist, Fred Fiedler, observed, "There are almost as many definitions of leadership as there are leadership theories—and there are almost as many theories of leadership as there are psychologists working in the field."

The reason that there is almost no agreement among leadership advice givers on a single definition of "effective leadership" is that each different "type" of follower and "type" of leadership advice giver looks for different qualities and behaviors in what they deem "effective leaders."

This is because all followers and all advice-givers have one of four different worldviews. I will introduce these worldviews as a central part of my model in later chapters. Here I will mention that leadership advice is often bogus because instead of one definition of effective leadership, there are actually four definitions. Each of the four leadership paradigms (that I will describe in this book) has its own definition of effective leadership. Each definition of "effective leadership" essentially amounts to pushing their own unconscious worldview bias as a one-size-fits-all definition of how all leaders should approach the practice of leadership.

Few if any leadership advice-givers contextualize their definition of effective leadership by saying, this is a definition of effective leadership for "traditional types" for "postmodern" or "progressive" types, or for "achiever" types. Rather, they just push their unconscious worldview bias and suggest their definition of effective leadership (for one of the worldviews) is the most effective way to lead all four types of followers. This of course is untrue, but that doesn't stop them from saying it.

It is no exaggeration to say that the advice-givers in the leadership industry have failed to provide a definition or description of effective leadership that they can agree to.
Barbara Kellerman, a Harvard professor, takes it one step further when she says, "the leadership industry has failed."

She is one of the few honest leadership professors who doesn't pull punches. She is a distinguished professor at Harvard University's John F. Kennedy School of Government. She was the Founding Executive Director at Harvard's Kennedy School's Center for Public Leadership, and previously served as the Director of the Center for the Advanced Study of Leadership at the Academy of Leadership at the University of Maryland. Kellerman has written a series of books that amount to scathing take downs of the bogus leadership industry including *Bad Leadership*, *The End of Leadership*, and *Professionalizing Leadership*.

In *The End of Leadership*, she describes how, despite the countless leadership programs, courses, seminars, trainers, consultants and coaches claiming to teach people how to lead, there is "scant evidence" that this enormous investment of time and money has paid off. (The leadership development industry is estimated to be $15 billion annually in the U.S. and $50 billion worldwide.)

In her follow-up book, *Professionalizing Leadership*, she notes that since the publishing of the End of Leadership in 2012, she is no longer alone in beginning to blow the whistle on these unethical practices such as trying to teach a complex and technical skill in a two-week seminar (which is what most of them do). "Since then, I have been joined by a small but fierce cadre of others who point to the yawning gap between what the leadership industry claims to do, and what it does."

Kellerman is joined by Stanford's Jeffrey Pfeffer as respected academics, thoughtful intellectuals, and true insiders who have recently turned leadership industry "whistleblowers."

Pfeffer, a prominent Stanford business school professor, and author of numerous books on management and leadership, including *Leadership* BS, writes "The single biggest barrier to effective leadership is, in my view, the leadership industry itself. Instead of telling people the skills and behaviors they need to be effective in getting things done, we tell them almost the opposite–blandishments about how we wish people would be, and how we wish workplaces were."

Pfeffer states flatly "The leadership industry has failed. It's not just that all the efforts to develop better leaders have failed to appreciably improve leadership, but they often make things much worse."

Finally, leadership researcher and New York Times bestselling author Duff McDonald, describes the leadership industry this way, "Most of it is bullshit. Unfortunately, there are few business school faculty who could ever summon the courage to admit such a thing. But some do, and using the same language."

I will reserve a more in-depth analysis of how and why the vast majority of leadership development investments are a waste of time and money for my other book, which I hope you will read, *Blowing the Whistle on Bogus Leadership: Veteran Insider Reveals Why 80% of All Leadership Trainings Are Complete Waste of Money.*

For our purposes here, I want to highlight three crucial facts in this whole sordid affair that is the leadership training and coaching industry.

First, the vast majority of so-called leadership experts, trainers and coaches do not know the answers to the most basic questions about leadership: What is leadership? How does leadership work? How can you develop leadership ability?

Second, as I explained above, none of the leadership experts can agree on which approach or style works best. In fact, about 90% of leadership advice-givers will tell you that the style they advocate is the "best" style and should pretty much be used with all people and circumstances.

Finally, as I mentioned already, and will explain in more detail later in this book, the reason that the experts can't agree on the above fundamentals is because they are "subject to their own worldview bias." I will explain this in more detail later, but this essentially means that they are unaware of their assumptions and biases about human psychology, human motivation, and follower needs and behavior.

My colleagues and I were the first to notice (and teach and write about) this pattern, thanks to the guidance of my mentor Ken Wilber. This pattern, definitively explains why there are so many definitions and descriptions of "effective" leadership that wildly contradict each other to the point of often being mutually exclusive.

This is why, as you will see shortly, worldviews are right at the center of my model of leadership. And the different leadership approaches (or styles as they can be called) that each of the four worldviews expects from legitimate and credible leaders (in their eyes) is also at the center of my model.

This is what makes it universal. Rather than a one-size-fits-all approach that amounts to pushing one's unconscious worldview bias, this model accounts for the different worldviews, needs and preferences of the followers, and accounts for the four universal leadership styles seen in nearly all leadership theory literature and leadership research.

My books are the first books ever published that connect these four universal worldviews with the four universal leadership styles. This connection forms the heart of the Unifying Theory of Leadership" that I developed with Ken Wilber at the Integral Institute in the early 2000s. This "meta theory" of leadership explains which leadership approaches (or styles) will work with which people and circumstances, and which approaches will be disastrous with which people and circumstances.

This leadership model is also unique in that it is the first to break down the complex skill of leadership into three "essential abilities" and nine essential leadership practices.

In a later chapter I will outline the four different definitions of "effective leadership" that the four different camps of leadership advice-givers offer (which reflect their unconscious worldview bias).

For now, it is useful to offer a stripped down, you could say generic or "worldview agnostic" definition free of the ubiquitous unconscious worldview bias.

> *Lead-er-ship (n): the ability or activity of inspiring and/or influencing people in relationship, over time, toward shared goals.*

The prerequisite for leadership is an established, trust-based relationship with followers who are voluntarily participating in activities toward shared goals over time.

If any of the prerequisite elements of *trust, relationship, voluntary participation, shared goals* or *time* are missing, it is definitely not leadership.

It might be *coercion, manipulation or authority*, but none of those meet the widely understood and accepted requirements to be considered "leadership."

The word "leadership" implies a trust-based relationship over time with shared goals, and the word "follower" implies voluntary participation. Remember that followership is voluntary. A follower chooses to see a person as their leader, and that can be revoked (by the follower) at any time.

In the case of an authority figure compelling them to comply with their order, a follower provides discretionary effort, which is effort above and beyond what would be considered compliance.

So when influence occurs inside the context of a leader-follower relationship, the follower is voluntarily participating in being influenced. Put another way, followers actually want the leader to influence them. Followers give the leader consent to influence them.

Bringing all of this together, we can think of "leadership influence" as *affecting a follower in a way that they voluntarily change how they think or behave.*

The next big idea I want to highlight in this chapter lies at the very heart of why 80% of leadership development efforts fail, and why so much of leadership theory and so much leadership advice, is so utterly bogus.

This may strike you as a little bit provocative, controversial or in the worst case even condescending. But it's really none of those things if you hear me out and grasp the nuance of the reality I'm pointing out for you. So bear with me and you will be glad that you did.

Many leadership trainers and coaches talk about leadership as if it is about personality traits, or qualities or vague concepts like "EQ" (more on this later).

While these topics are interesting in the background, discussing these topics do next to nothing to help leaders actually improve their leadership performance.

Improving leadership performance has little to do with concepts and everything to do with skill.

The vast majority of leadership trainers and coaches seem to be ignorant of the relatively obvious and definitely indisputable fact that *leadership is a technical and complex skill.*

> *There is only one way to learn a technical and / or complex skill. That is to train in the specific, requisite techniques until they are internalized as habits, then layer on more techniques to create skills, then combine several new skills to create new "skill sets" and ultimately those skill sets mature into what we call "abilities."*

This crucial point is a central element in my rapid leadership development methodology and is the subject of the next section of this introduction (and the subject of my four-book series called "Accelerating Leadership").

To get better at leadership, you must understand the nature of leadership. Leadership is not a set of personality traits and it is not some vague concept (although many authors, trainers and coaches speak about it as though it is).

> *Leadership is a technical and complex skill, no different from all the many other technical and complex skills you have already learned both as a child and as an adult*

You know this intuitively, but for some odd reason, most leadership authors, trainers and coaches don't seem to.

> *Learning the technical and complex skill of leadership is no different than learning any of those other technical and complex skills that you already took the time to learn. The method is exactly the same*

Yet less than 10% of leadership development programs use it. Learning leadership is exactly the same as learning to play a musical instrument, mastering a martial art or sport, flying an airplane or any other technical and/or complex skill.

How could it be otherwise?

The Universal Leadership Model reflects this fact and therefore emphasizes "practices" (which can also be thought of as techniques or behaviors).

Any proposed model of leadership that fails to point to the techniques and practices that comprise the technical and complex skill called "leadership" is flawed from the start.

This is such an important point, I am going to revisit it several times in this book coming at it from a variety of different angles and using different analogies. Please pardon my deliberate repetition, but if there is one thing

you must understand, it is this. And I don't want you to just be familiar with it as a concept, I want you to believe it and understand it in your bones. Once you do, all of your future leadership development efforts (and the efforts in your organization) will be much easier and much more effective. This is one of the main things I want you to get out of this short book.

Let me explain in very concrete terms that will make this easy to grasp. I will refer to several common technical and complex skills. I'm confident that you are very familiar with one or two of them and this will help you understand.

No one in their right mind would try to learn to play an instrument, try to learn a martial art, or try to learn to fly an airplane the way 90% of leadership development programs train leadership.

> *Can you imagine trying to learn to play the guitar by reading case studies of great guitar players in history, or worse, hearing stories about the accomplishments of great guitarists, or worse still, reading a list of character traits of these men and women? Can you imagine trying to learn Kung Fu by hearing stories about Bruce Lee, descriptions of his personality traits or by merely adopting his mindset or philosophy?*

As absurd as this sounds, it is even more absurd that this is exactly what approximately 90% of leadership development programs are doing in the $15 billion-a-year leadership development industry (in the United States alone with an estimated $50 billion worldwide).

My team and I have been creating and delivering successful leadership development programs for over two decades, and I am now calling out these bogus industry practices.

Research shows clearly that programs that emphasize leadership qualities, traits, philosophy, and case studies (instead of techniques and practices) fail to help leaders improve their leadership skills or their leadership performance.

I want you to pause for a moment and imagine signing up your son or daughter to a training to learn to play piano and asking them what techniques your child will be practicing each week. Now imagine that their answer is, "Our students don't practice any specific techniques. Our students study the 'qualities' of great piano players."

There is an entire field called "Complex Skill Instructional Design." Google it. It is a very well-known fact in training and development that in order to learn any technical or complex skill, you must break the overall ability down into specific skill sets and skills, and then down to the techniques that make up those skills. This is common sense. You already know this.

We can use the complex skill called baseball as a simple example.

Many children learn this complex skill. Perhaps you did. When you (or your child or niece or nephew) learned the ability to play baseball, it was broken down to *throwing, catching, hitting the ball, and running the bases.*

In the case of basketball, it is *dribbling, passing, shooting* and *rebounding.*

In the case of mixed martial arts, it is *wrestling, kick-boxing* and *grappling.*

There is also a well-known field called "Expert Performance Theory" or "Deliberate Practice" (as it is better known). You have no doubt heard of "10,000 hours" as the estimated amount of time it takes for a person practicing deliberately to go from beginner to expert level in any complex skill.

Why don't leadership development programs incorporate "Deliberate Practice" into their efforts and teach their students the practices (the techniques and skills) that leaders need to be effective?

My partners, colleagues and I have been teaching the complex skill called "leadership" using "complex skill instructional design" and "deliberate practice" for more than 20 years. I have logged more than 20,000 hours doing precisely that. So, let me save you a lot of time, energy, money and

heartburn and tell you what does not work and exactly what does actually work for leadership development.

Leadership, like any other complex skill, is made up of a specific set of skills with discrete, concrete behaviors that can be practiced, repeated, and internalized as habits.

Again, using baseball as a familiar example, you have to be able to throw, hit, run, and do several other skills before you have the ability that we call "baseball." The same goes for martial arts, music, flying an airplane and leadership.

> *There is only one way to learn a complex skill: practice and internalize a technique, then combine several techniques (in layers) over time.*

This is called "complex skill instructional design" and "deliberate practice." It is also called "common sense."

We all instinctively understand that learning a complex skill involves breaking the broader ability down into smaller skill sets and skills, then teaching those specific techniques and behaviors. We all used this same method when we learned to read, when we learned mathematics, when we took music lessons, and when we began our career.

Clearly, to learn (or improve) this ability called leadership, it must be broken down into specific skill sets and discrete techniques (behaviors).

Think about mixed martial arts (MMA). There are three major abilities (*wrestling, kick-boxing and grappling*) and each is made up of a dozen or so techniques. The fact that MMA athletes have separate training and separate coaches for wrestling, boxing and grappling underscores the nature of this complex ability (which has many parallels to leadership, which is obviously at least as complex as martial arts).

Revealing My Trade Secret

I want to share the unique mechanism that my partners, employees and students have been using for 22 years to get 3X to 5X better results (in terms of leadership skill improvement) over conventional leadership education practices. It is this:

> *We teach leadership as a practice made up of concrete, specific discreet techniques. We do not emphasize concepts (much less vague "qualities"); rather, we focus on the specific techniques that are combined to create skills (which in turn are combined to create the common skill sets we know effective leaders use universally). While we do draw on best practices, we contextualize those techniques to make sure we are using the right approach with the right people and circumstances.*

The Universal Leadership Model described in this book reflects these crucial distinctions.

Leadership as Deliberate Practice

"Deliberate practice" is the method that surgeons, professional athletes, peak performers (and the 10,000+ leaders who have attended my trainings) use to quickly learn and internalize new skills.

My partners and I have used this method for 20+ years, helping leaders rapidly adopt new skills with consistent results. I can summarize deliberate practice with three main elements:

1) *You must train "technique"*

To learn a complex skill efficiently, you must isolate the techniques that make up the skill, set specific goals based on best practices and benchmarks, practice daily (or at least weekly) with full attention and push beyond your comfort zone.

2) *You must receive expert mentorship to ensure that you are practicing the techniques correctly*

This looks like frequent coaching and guidance from people who have mastered the technique and know how to teach it. Facilitators and coaches must be experts in the specific techniques (not merely mindsets).

3) *You must obtain feedback to calibrate and improve*

This aspect of deliberate practice involves obtaining immediate feedback (from qualified experts) to be able to calibrate and fine tune the technique as you internalize and habitualize it. The first technique has to be correct before layering on the one that comes next. And the next has to be correct before layering on the one that follows.

This is the essence of "Practice Based Leadership" which is the method that I invented 22 years ago.

I am not going to mince words here. Do not spend another dollar with so-called leadership development experts who aren't experts in the specific leadership techniques that you need to learn to improve your skills!

> *You would never hire a guitar teacher or a baseball coach who can't play guitar or who isn't a terrific baseball player, or who doesn't know which techniques to teach you, or who wastes your time talking to you about the "qualities" of great guitar players or baseball players*

Don't hire leadership trainers or coaches who do that either!

To break it down further into the techniques, you wouldn't go into a baseball "batting cage" to train on that skill with someone who is a "mindset coach" or "life coach" or "executive coach" who has never swung a bat (much less possesses the expert level proficiency of doing the technique perfectly).

> *Imagine a martial arts or baseball coach who only talked to you about mindset and asked you a lot of reflection questions but didn't teach you how to correctly practice your new techniques, or worse, didn't even know the techniques in the first place?*

Kind of obvious when you think about it, right?

Repetition is the mother of skill. So I will repeat this crucial point one more time

> *The only effective way to learn technical and complex skills (baseball, basketball, playing a musical instrument, martial arts, flying an airplane or leadership) is to break the ability down into its component parts or "skills" and then train, memorize, internalize, and then layer the techniques until they become second nature.*

Learning complex skills follows a pattern that looks like this. (Again, you already know this because you have already mastered numerous complex skills. So let me remind you what you already know.)

1. Over many weeks, practices become habits.

2. Over many months, habits become skills.

3. With time and ongoing practice, those skills combine into "skill sets."

4. Ultimately, the skill sets come together to form the "ability" (the complex skill) that the learner is practicing.

To be competent at baseball, an athlete must have the skills to throw, catch, hit and run. To be competent at MMA, an athlete must have wrestling, kick-boxing, and grappling skills.

For the past 22+ years, all of my leadership trainings have used "Deliberate Practice" principles from "Expert Performance Theory."

This is central to why my leadership trainings consistently produce results where most leadership training programs fail. And as you will soon discover, this essential design principle is "baked in" to the Universal Leadership Model.

As mentioned prior, the person who pioneered much of the research in this area and coined the term "Deliberate Practice" was Anders Ericsson. He has written several books, but I will highlight two here. They are: *The Cambridge Handbook of Expertise and Expert Performance and Peak: Secrets from the New Science of Expertise.*

We will use Anders Ericsson's own words to define and clarify exactly what deliberate practice is...

> *"Deliberate practice develops skills that other people have already figured out how to do and for which effective training techniques have been established. The practice regimen should be designed and overseen by a teacher or coach who is familiar with the abilities of expert performers and with how those abilities can best be developed."*

This is why I will frequently remind you throughout this book that the fastest way to learn leadership skills is to get mentoring, guidance and coaching from people who are experts in those specific techniques. To truly understand a skill, it's not enough to just hear about it or read about it, you must experience it and practice it over and over until it becomes habit. This is one of the main reasons that most leadership development programs fail to develop leaders. They usually teach the wrong things in the wrong way. If they aren't teaching specific skills then they aren't actually helping people get better at the technical and complex skill called leadership.

To progress in your leadership skills, your facilitators and coaches must be experts in both the techniques they are teaching and the best methods to teach those techniques. If their "leadership model" does not emphasize specific techniques and practices, and if their advice to help leaders get better at the technical and complex skill of leadership does not incorporate "deliberate practice," then I strongly suggest you look elsewhere.

Further, if your leadership trainer or coach is not a "black belt" (an expert) in the techniques they are coaching you in, then they are not qualified to coach you. If you spend money on leadership coaches who are not experts in the specific skills of leadership, then you are wasting your time and your money. And this includes the ubiquitous "mindset coaches" who will happily take your money but can't teach you anything about leadership. People who say "mindset is everything" don't know much about anything. Mindset is most definitely not everything. It's not even the main thing. Mindset is 20% at most. Strategy and technique are 80% or more of what leads to success in any endeavor.

> *Mindset coaching is mainly helpful for experts who already know how to do a technique perfectly and are trying to adopt the best psychology (mindset) to help them do it more consistently.*

Mindset coaching is great for professional athletes who are already at the very top of their game and who know the techniques well. Executive coaches and self-described leadership coaches who focus primarily on mindset, in my experience, do this because they do not know the strategies, skills or techniques of leadership.

In my opinion, if they did know the techniques of leadership, they would be sharing them with their clients (a lot more than mindset). To be blunt, focusing on mindset is a primary way that unqualified leadership coaches cover up their lack of knowledge about leadership. Do them a favor and share this book with them. Maybe they will choose to level up their knowledge about leadership.

Hopefully, after reading this introduction, you are eager to see the model and learn how to start applying it in your own leadership and leadership development efforts. Our next step is to have at least a basic understanding of leadership theory. We will cover that next in Chapter 2

CHAPTER 2: LEADERSHIP THEORY PRIMER

Abraham Maslow famously stated, "If the only tool you have is a hammer, you tend to see every problem as a nail." When you begin to wade into the field of "Leadership Theory and Practice," you will find a large body of information coming from various schools of thought, each asserting the "right" way to lead. Each of these "schools of thought," riddled with bias and once-size-fits-all thinking, advocates their specific leadership approach, often as "the best way" (or even the only legitimate way) that leaders should lead.

There's the *"Hammer" School* ... the *"Plier" School* ... *the "Screwdriver" School* ...

Some schools of thought emphasize the character traits of the leader. Others emphasize leadership best practices. Each "school" offers incomplete truths that do, in fact, work some of the time when paired with the right people and circumstances, however, almost none of them tell you which people and circumstances!

Worse, when paired with the wrong people, their singular approach often backfires spectacularly, destroying the leader's credibility while demoralising the team.

If you've read a dozen books on leadership you may think, "Wow, it seems like none of these people can agree on what leadership is, how it works, or how to develop it."

If you do think that, you are right.

The leadership theory primer in this chapter will explain why that is the case, and will offer something few of the other "experts" offer: *a coherent explanation of how these diverse leadership theories fit together and a framework that can be universally applicable across leader/follower contexts.*

It is helpful to ground this discussion in your own experience. So I will invite you to think about your own experience with leaders and the different approaches they take to leadership.

It's likely that you have worked around leaders who are goal-oriented, aims to find the highest-leverage strategies, and find ways to incentivize bright people to execute using those strategies. These incentives often boil down to more money or more organizational influence. While this style of leadership works well with certain people, it can be ineffective with others. You might even have heard these leaders complain that the younger generation lacks "motivation" because the financial incentives being offered don't seem to interest them.

At some point in your career, you may also have worked for a boss with a different approach. Perhaps this leader firmly adhered to the "chain of command." These types of leaders follow a strict hierarchy of authority. They give clear instructions and expect compliance from the people "under them." Once in a position of authority, they assume a kind of "parental" orientation toward those who report to them. While this style of leadership works extremely well with some followers, others may find its hierarchical nature to be off-putting and the strict "top-down" mentality to be too rigid.

Perhaps you've also worked with leaders (or read books by authors) who emphasize the concept of "self-managed teams," giving everyone a voice and striving for consensus, and treating everyone as an equal. From this point of view, leadership does not come from a single individual, but rather, it emerges collectively as a result of shared values and vision, open dialogue, and mutual trust. While this collaborative, self-managed approach can work with some people, it can be confusing and even demoralizing to those who don't want to strive for consensus but simply want the boss to tell them what to do.

When you survey the leadership literature, you will recognize these very different approaches to leadership usually recommended as the "one best way" to lead that should be used in every context with all followers.

These leadership advice-givers are often biased by their own narrow worldview that they make the huge ethnocentric assumption that all employees have a similar mindset (worldview) and prefer that style of leadership. Again, this strikes me as naive. It suggests they have made no effort to learn about developmental psychology and have no grasp of the diversity of mindsets / worldviews in the workplace.

In addition to the many "leadership experts" who advocate their singular approach to leading, there are also many textbooks written over many decades about this topic which is referred to as "leadership theory and practice." The countless versions of college textbooks with titles similar to "Handbook of Leadership Theory and Practice" provide surveys and summaries of the many theories and practices of leadership.

Almost all of these textbooks lack any kind of credible or compelling unifying thesis or leadership model. These books are like a buffet of different theories and views of leadership, however very few of them attempt to synthesize these together into a coherent map or model of some kind.

This may come as a surprise to you, given what a central, significant topic it is. The reasons why no one (until now) has attempted, much less succeeded, in this task will become clear as you read this chapter.

My mentor and colleague Ken Wilber noticed the same problem in the early 2000s. There was no "unifying theory of leadership" of any kind (that would pass even the slightest sniff test for being comprehensive or accurate).

There were (and are) thousands of practices and hundreds of theories. While every theorist and advocate of leadership had an opinion about what leadership is, how it works, and how to develop it, none of them agreed!

> *Nearly all theories and models of leadership contradict many, if not most, of the other theories and models. What conclusion should we draw from this? A less generous conclusion is that leadership theory is basically bullshit.*

And that would be an understandable conclusion for someone who takes the time to read the opinions of these so-called "leadership experts" as I have. Back in 2003, at the Integral Institute, my mentor offered me a kinder, and more generous frame.

Ken asked me, *"Brett, what if they are all right, but they are also all partial, and incomplete? What if they all have a piece of the puzzle of what constitutes effective leadership but simply lack an adequate big-picture framework that explains under what circumstances and with which people these leadership approaches will be effective?"*

Ken continued, *"What if each theorist is 'right' in the sense that the approaches they advocate are effective? It's just that their assumptions about who those approaches will be effective with haven't been fully fleshed out? Could it be possible that all of their approaches might be effective if they could be correctly paired with the people and circumstances they are most suitable for?"*

As you perhaps can imagine, my initial reaction was a sense of possibility that quickly turned to overwhelm.

There are hundreds of leadership theories and thousands of management and leadership practices that would have to be accounted for! The number of people and circumstances to pair them with would be nearly limitless!

How could we possibly uncover a single unifying principle that underlies and explains all leader and follower needs, motivations and behaviors?

And how could one unifying theory weave together the hundreds of diverse leadership theories, that many cases, says the very opposite and contradicts the other established theories.

To even attempt such an ambitious understanding, some kind of robust, reliable framework for human consciousness and behaviour would be required, one that could accurately explain and predict human motivation and behaviour across hundreds of cultures over the thousands of years that these leadership practices (and theories) have been developed.

I don't recall exactly how I articulated this dilemma to Ken back in 2003, but I do recall the look on his face.

It conveyed something like, "Well duh."

And it was in that moment that the trajectory of my career changed.

I got it!

Over nearly 100 years, integral theory had already painstakingly aggregated all major fields of social science, psychology and philosophy and synthesized them together into an over-arching framework that accurately accounted for all human motivation, mental models, worldviews and behavior patterns.

That was what drew me to Ken Wilber's work, and to Integral Institute in the first place.

> *Surely somewhere in this collection of "integral maps" there must be some orienting generalizations that can help us synthesize all of these contradictory leadership theories into something that shows which of these numerous approaches will work best with which people and circumstances*

That began a decade-long crusade to "crack the code of leadership" that lasted from 2003 to 2013. The goal was to figure out if there could be a Unifying Theory of Leadership that is true and reliable across all human contexts and also could contextualize each of the hundreds of theories (and thousands of practices) and could, in effect, breathe new life into old and largely outdated theories by pointing out the precise people and circumstances those approaches will, in fact, work well in.

I spent many years traveling back and forth between Texas and Colorado dividing my time between the integral think tank crowd of mentors and colleagues in Colorado, and my leadership academy in Texas where I had the laboratory, budget and staff to experiment with these new hypotheses with C-Suite executives and their organizations.

It took a year or two of trial and error, and there are some hilarious stories of early failed experiments that my business partner (and dear friend) Rand Stagen and I like to tell, but I will save those for future books.

Soon we discovered the unlocking key that was right under our noses all along.

Ken Wilber's integral maps feature dimensions of human experience and categories of common worldviews that held the key that would unlock our elusive "Unifying Theory of Leadership."

Once we applied these integral frameworks as sort of a meta map, or overlay, every one of the hundreds of leadership theories (and thousands of practices) easily clicked right into place, seamlessly. Eureka!

A More Nuanced Understanding of Leadership

Leadership theories appear to seek to answer the question, "Why are some leaders successful, while others fail?"

Leadership is many things, but it all boils down to a relationship between two or more people and how they coordinate their efforts over time to accomplish a shared goal.

Zooming out to the essence of organisational leadership, organisational leaders must... 1) set the goal and develop a plan, 2) pull together a group of engaged and motivated individuals who can coordinate their efforts to complete the work, and 3) ensure that the plan is successfully implemented.

Given this obvious reality, is quite accurate and also useful to say that, in its most essential form, organizational leadership is a function of three things: *planning, teaming, and executing.*

At the very minimum, there is the "leader" and the "follower." Or stated without the concrete suggestion of durable "roles" we might say there is the person "who is engaging in activities" we associate with "leading" and there is the person "engaging in activities" we associate with "following." There is a strongly implied relationship dynamic between these two (or more) people.

That "interpersonal dynamic" between these two (or more) people is what we are pointing at when we use the word "leadership."

I can offer some clarity by saying that leadership is an interpersonal phenomenon. I like to describe organizational leadership as "interpersonal psychology at scale."

So, for us to begin to have a good grasp on leadership and how the different leadership theories can be useful, we must ground our exploration on the fact that there are two or more people interacting, and there is a relationship and a relationship dynamic between them, and finally, that interaction / relationship is occurring in a specific set of circumstances (or context).

So to summarize, we have the "leader," the "follower(s)," and the circumstances.

This dimension we call "leadership circumstances" and "context" bears special emphasis.

As you may have noticed when reading leadership books or working with leadership coaches), many emphasize traits or qualities (or strengths) of leaders. I will return to this central issue with conventional leadership training and coaching repeatedly throughout this book.

This over-emphasis on the "qualities" of the leader represents a major failure to recognize the critical importance of the context in which the leader is relating and behaving. Different contexts require different approaches to leadership and relationships. A person whose leadership is viewed as disastrous would likely be seen as a brilliant leader in a different context. This crucial topic will be unpacked further in later chapters of this book.

For now, please realize that the context in which the leader is relating and behaving largely determines the "meaning" of the leader's behaviors and therefore is at least as, if not more, important than the leader's qualities.

Finally, by way of introduction—and this turned out to be the key to cracking the code on leadership theory—is that in order to adequately understand a given leadership theory, you must take into consideration the assumptions, the values and beliefs, in short, the "worldview" of the theorist who posited the theory.

While this is now clear to me as a result of my collaboration with Ken Wilber, the following insight does not occur to most people.

Every person who has ever proposed a "theory of leadership" has certain beliefs, values, and assumptions. Put another way, every leadership theorist has a specific view of the world (worldview), and as you would expect, those assumptions about the "people" and "circumstances" significantly influence their theories of leadership.

Simply, a person's assumptions about people and what motivates them heavily influence their point of view of what leadership is and how it works with people.

As we saw earlier in this chapter, it also creates blind spots as a result of the naive assumption that all people will respond positively to leadership approaches that may, in fact, only work with a small group of people who share the theorist's worldview.

This applies to every single leadership theory (and theorist) in history and up to the present time.

Katzenbach and Smith, who created the self-managed team's approach, what we call "humanistic" leadership (or "collaborative" leadership), have a very different worldview and mindset than Ken Blanchard who created the very simplistic, step-by-step, rule-based One Minute Manager Approach.

As a result of them having different views of the world, they make very different assumptions about the psychological makeup of the people in a given organization.

There is the phrase, *preaching to the choir*. Well these different authors are preaching to very different choirs.

To illustrate this crucial principle, we can take a well-known leadership theory called "Leadership Theory X and Leadership Theory Y." This is a commonly-used example in the literature, so you may already be familiar with it. These two early theories of leadership were popularized in the 1950s. This juxtaposition describes two contrasting sets of assumptions that

leaders make about their followers (you can also say that "managers" make about their "employees").

Leaders who subscribe to "Theory X" hold a worldview and a set of assumptions and beliefs about people that can be summarized as "people dislike work, have little ambition, and are unwilling to take responsibility."

Leaders who subscribe to "Theory Y" hold a worldview and a set of assumptions and beliefs about people that can be summarized as "People are generally self-motivated and tend to enjoy the challenge of work."

It should be obvious that a leader who subscribes to the Theory X worldview will approach leadership and relationships with followers very differently than a leader who subscribes to Theory Y.

It is very important to understand that each leader / manager holds a worldview (with inherent assumptions and beliefs about people and circumstances) that informs everything they do and think in their role as manager or leader.

Applying this insight turned out to be the key to cracking the code on a "unifying theory of leadership."

I will break it down to make it simple.

Every person has a worldview, sometimes called a "value system," that plays a central role in how they make meaning of their experiences. A person's worldview acts as a kind of filter that helps people interpret the meaning of their experiences.

This makes intuitive sense if you think about it. In fact, how could it be otherwise?

What is far less intuitive, and took my research team at Integral Institute a few years to recognize, even under the helpful mentorship and direction of Ken Wilber, was that the leadership scholars, professors and textbook authors were no exception to this rule.

The theorists were also subject to their own biases, and those assumptions about people (and the world) not only were implicated in their theories, they essentially defined them!

These leadership theorists interpreted all of the facts and data, as well as their leadership research, through the lens of their worldview (which varies from theorist to theorist). This realization was the key to understanding over 100 years of leadership theory.

For our purposes here, I will keep this brief and reveal the single crucial pattern that made a unifying theory of leadership possible.

Once you recognize the assumptions and beliefs inherent in the worldview of the theorist, each leadership theory starts to make a whole lot more sense. And while that set of assumptions and beliefs (worldview) may make a given leadership theory partial, flawed, impractical (or even doomed to failure) with certain people and circumstances, it gives us clues as to where that approach may work really well: with people who share the theorists' worldview.

Put succinctly, when we understand worldviews, it gives us unambiguous, helpful clues about which people and circumstances a given leadership theory are actually quite likely to work very well!

We will start by summarizing the main approaches to leadership theories that provide the backbone of our academic understanding of leadership.

To help make this easier to understand, I will use the convention of time (oldest theories first) as well as the main "worldviews" (assumptions and beliefs about the world and the people in it) that these theories reflect.

If you have ever perused the endless listing of leadership-related books in Amazon, or if you have read college textbooks on leadership with names like "The Handbook of Leadership Theory and Practice" (there are hundreds of these) ... then you are familiar with the numerous different leadership theories (and theorists), most of which contradict each other. It is not an exaggeration to say that the field of leadership theory is an overwhelming, confusing, mess.

To help create some order out of this chaos, I developed some useful "lenses" with which we can look through and see these theories in a context that makes logical sense.

It is useful to have some categories to place these numerous leadership theories into. As mentioned before, most books and textbooks either offer their "one way to lead" viewpoint or they offer a hodgepodge "buffet" of different approaches to leadership, but rarely (if ever), do they tell you which approaches to use with which people and circumstances.

To reduce the clutter and not be overwhelmed by these numerous theories, we can place them into four broad categories based on their "view" of leadership (what they see and emphasize): *the Trait View, the Behavioral View, the Styles view and the Circumstances view.*

1. The Trait View of Leadership

So-called "Trait Theories" ask the question, "What personality traits make a good leader?"

This approach to leadership theory assumes that effective leaders share a number of personality characteristics or "traits." These characteristics or traits are also sometimes referred to as "qualities."

While you may already recognize some inherent limitations in this assumption, you should know that this is still a very popular approach to leadership and leadership development. A surprisingly large number of leadership training and coaching programs focus on these characteristics, traits or qualities of a leader. As you might imagine, this is extremely ineffective and rarely produces significant gains in leadership skills or capabilities, yet it is still a very popular, albeit ineffective, approach.

These "trait theories" are sometimes referred to as "early theories" and often assume that leadership is an innate, instinctive quality of a person's character. Put simply, this is the "leaders are born, not made" view of leadership.

Some examples of the character traits that these theories point to include: integrity, empathy, influence, judgment, charisma, confidence, and so on.

Trait theories are generally ineffective in terms of developing leadership skills (leadership capability) because personality traits cannot be learned, however, having a list of these "qualities" at least provides a kind of developmental vision or a picture of the type of person one aspires to be like. Perhaps it offers the learner some motivation to study leadership so that they can somehow become more like leaders who have these innate traits.

Besides the obvious fact that a student of leadership can't learn a character trait, the other huge limitation is that trait theories tend to completely ignore context.

Put another way, even if a person has these traits innately, they do not guarantee success because it is based on the assumption that these traits work with all people in every circumstance, an assumption that is obviously false.

Different people in different circumstances will respond quite differently to a leader's personality traits (or qualities). A particular leadership approach may be extremely effective in one set of circumstances and people and extremely disastrous in a different set of circumstances with different people.

2. The Behavioral View of Leadership

The next lens is the so-called "Behavioral Theories" which ask the question, "What do effective leaders do?"

As the name suggests, these behavioral theories focus on how leaders behave. For example, does the leader give orders or direct followers to do things (and assume compliance) or does the leader take an indirect approach by inquiring into the followers' perspectives about the project and discussing and deciding together what should be done next. Does the leader make the decision herself or himself, or does the leader encourage the followers to participate in the decision-making process? Does the leader select the vision / destination then instruct followers what to do, or does the leader invite the followers into a shared visioning process?

In the 1930s, behavioral theorist Kurt Lewin developed a framework that is well-known and still often quoted today. It suggests that there are three categories of leaders, the "Autocratic," "Democratic," and Laissez Faire."

According to Lewin, "Autocratic leaders" make decisions without consulting their teams. Lewin viewed this style of leadership as most appropriate when decisions need to be made quickly, when there's no need for input from followers, and when collective team agreement is not necessary for a successful outcome.

On the other hand, "Democratic" leaders solicit input from the followers before making a decision, although the degree of input can vary from leader to leader. Lewin believes that this style is important when team agreement does matter to the outcome. He acknowledges the fact that this process can be difficult to manage when there are a lot of different perspectives to take into account.

There is a third broad category of leaders who don't fit into either of the above due to the fact that they don't exert any influence at all on the decisions their followers are making. Lewin describes "Laissez-faire" leaders as not interfering. The French phrase "Laissez-faire" when translated into English means "allow to do." It is defined as, "Letting things take their own course, without interfering."

Some people say, "hands off" leadership. Laissez-faire leaders allow people within the team to make many of the decisions on their own. Lewin believes that this works well when a team is highly competent, is self-motivated, and doesn't require close supervision to achieve a successful outcome.

Workers who have a strong desire for autonomy and are sensitive to feeling "micromanaged" in any way may appreciate this more hands-off leadership style. Perhaps in the 1930's, Lewin was already anticipating many aspects of the now-popular (with postmodern thinkers' (and the "woke" Gen Xers and Millennials, as they are often called) style of leadership referred to as "self-managed teams."

However, a less generous interpretation of this "Laissez-faire" leadership approach may simply be a result of the fact that the leader is busy, preoccupied with other priorities, distracted, lazy or in the worst case, really doesn't care about the team, the individuals on the team or the outcome.

"Laissez-faire" leadership often fails because, in a certain sense, it is not strictly leadership. It certainly wouldn't be considered "effective leadership" by most reasonable people. It's not a mischaracterization to say that "Laissez-faire" leaders are simply choosing "not to lead." From that point of view, "Laissez-faire" leadership is not an approach to leadership at all. It is an approach characterized by choosing to "not lead" or it is an "absence" of leadership.

Later theorists such as Blake and Mouton who introduced the "Blake-Mouton Managerial Grid" brings a more nuanced approach to behavioral theories by plotting "Concern for Results" (low to high) on an X-axis and "Concern for People" on a Y axis, which naturally produces four quadrants.

This convention has been widely adopted by behavioral theorists and might be more familiar as the "balancing task and relationship" trope. Perhaps the most popular evolution of this convention is the very widely used *Situational Leadership* model popularized by Ken Blanchard starting in the 1970s and up to today. In this iteration of the "managerial grid" concept, the X-axis becomes "Directive Behavior" and the Y axis becomes "Supportive Behavior" which again produces four quadrants (behaviors) labeled *Directing, Coaching, Supporting and Delegating.*

It's easy to see that these four behaviors are actually management behaviors and not leadership behaviors at all. In truth, this is a model of "situational management" but perhaps they figured they could sell more books if they called the model "Situational Leadership." We highlight it here because even today, this remains the most popular of the "behavioral leadership" theories.

To summarize, we have looked at the first two broad categories of leadership theories, the *Trait Theories and the Behavioral Theories* which emphasize the leader's character traits (or qualities) and the leader's behaviors.

You may notice that these first two lenses of leadership theory put very little emphasis on the followers. This is a major flaw in most of the early leadership theories. Rather than focus on the unique needs and preferences of the people being led (the followers), the focus of the research and recommendations remained squarely on the leader's traits and behavior.

3. The Styles View of Leadership

You can see how the arc of leadership thinking evolved over time, beginning with the psychologically unsophisticated, and you could even say that the somewhat naive notion of early leadership theories that leadership is fundamentally about the character traits of "great men," as the theories are sometimes referred to.

As the field of management and leadership theory moved into modern times, and benefitted from a less naive and more scientific view of psychology, the theories started looking more closely at behavior and relationships between leaders and followers. So we moved from the traditional trait theories to the more psychologically-savvy behavioral theories.

This leads us to the next major lens of leadership theory which we call the "Styles" view. You could fold this under the "Behavioral" view as Styles are, in essence, a group of behaviors. However, for our purposes here, it is more useful to take the Styles view out from the Behavioral view because it opens up many new possibilities that, when combined with a much more sophisticated understanding of psychology and context, can be put to good use to produce some of the latest and most useful leadership theories, practices and tools.

In simple terms, the Styles view of leadership recognizes that different people adopt a variety of "leadership styles" as a result of many factors, and innate personality traits is but one of those factors. Other factors that influence a person's leadership style include their various bits of intelligence (also known as lines of development). For example, a person who has a high IQ but a low EQ would develop a different style than a person with a very high EQ. A person who is more of a "thinker" would develop a different leadership style than a person who is less of a "thinker" and more of a "hands on, doer" type person.

Another differentiating factor is that it should be obvious to most thoughtful people that, just like in sports, or the arts, styles can be learned and can be adapted and evolved over time (because they are behaviors). And as we see in sports and in the arts, as practitioners cultivate greater versatility, they can even master more than one style and use different styles in different circumstances.

4. The Circumstances View of Leadership

After a few more decades, management science and leadership theory benefited from an even more sophisticated understanding of psychology and human behavior. With the advent of systems theory, theorists were able to apply a much more coherent understanding of the role that circumstance plays in leadership performance.

This reflects another important evolution in the thinking of leadership theorists. At this point in history, leadership theorists are starting to become more "context aware."

This brings us to the "Circumstances" view of leadership. These often go by the term "Contingency Theories." These theories ask the question, "How do the context and the circumstance influence leadership effectiveness?"

Contingency theorists realize that there is no one correct type of leader or style of leadership that works in every circumstance (no "one size fits all"), therefore, effective leadership is largely a function of the context in which leadership activities arise.

Contingency theories attempt to discern which leadership approach will work best in which circumstance. For example, which leadership approach is best when you need to make quick decisions, or when you need the full buy-in of every member of your team to achieve a successful outcome? Should a leader be more people-oriented or task-oriented in a given circumstance?

Systems theory, and in particular the field referred to as "situational awareness" takes circumstances into account.

One of the most important aspects of circumstances, which is sometimes underemphasized, is the role that the followers play in the circumstances. In a leader's circumstance or context, one of the most important aspects is the needs, values, worldviews, mindsets, styles and preferences of the followers and the teams the leader is supporting and attempting to influence.

This point will become extremely important as this training unfolds and you learn to expand your leadership versatility to be able to influence and motivate many different types of people, not just people who share your views and preferences.

It's not hard to see how leadership theory continually evolved from the very concrete and simplistic notions of personality traits, to progressively more nuanced theories that reflected a better understanding of behaviors and styles, eventually including the contexts in which those behaviors and styles might be more or less useful.

Survey of Some of the Most Popular Theories

To help you have a well-rounded and comprehensive understanding of leadership theory, I want to briefly mention some of the more popular theories that the theorists looking at leadership (through the various lenses) have produced and popularized. You will have heard of many of these theories (but perhaps not all of them). The reason I am going to do this is so you too can begin to see the pattern that my mentor Ken Wilber helped me and the team at Integral Institute uncover.

All of these theories are tied to the predominant worldview of the theorists who put them forth. Further, all of these leadership theories reflect the prevailing assumptions about followers. Each worldview, including the worldviews held by the theorists themselves, assumes different things about people, especially the psychological makeup of followers.

This will help you understand how all leadership theories and approaches can be plugged into my Universal Leadership Model which is tied to the worldviews of the followers, which we refer to as "follower mindsets."

Once you understand your organization's culture and your team members' predominant "follower mindsets," then you can refer to the theories and best practices that will in fact be very useful. And you will know which leadership theories and styles are not going to be useful because they will not work with your employees or followers.

Don't worry if this seems a little academic, or just out of reach at first because a lot of these concepts are new to you. As you continue through the book, everything will become crystal clear.

Looking back at how the prevailing views of leadership have evolved, we can recognize the "Four Fundamental Lenses of Leadership Theory" that have been introduced previously. These four lenses on leadership influenced theorists and the theories they advocated.

As a simple convention to organize this long list of theories into some kind of logical groupings, we will use the convention of time.

We will refer to these different time frames as *Imperial, Traditional, Modern and Postmodern* which we borrow from the fields of history, sociology and psychology.

By grouping these theories into these historical time frames, you will start to recognize the pattern.

These time frames sync up perfectly to the four fundamental worldviews which are identical to the four fundamental "follower mindsets." These terms also refer to "perspectives" or "worldviews."

All of these perspectives or worldviews are still very popular today. And they are very relevant because they make up the four possible follower mindsets that you will be encountering in your career as an organizational leader.

You are likely already familiar with these terms. It may be helpful to link them to the historical periods in which these worldviews first appeared.

The *Imperial* worldview (which is still very much alive and well today) first emerged in society during the time of feudal kingdoms and is roughly equivalent to the Bronze Age.

The *Traditional* worldview initially emerged with the monotheistic religious traditions and the Roman Empire, and we see it starting with the Iron Age (and continuing through the Middle Ages.)

The *Modern* worldview emerged during the historical western enlightenment and the dawn of scientific thinking we associate with "The Renaissance" which eventually led to the Industrial Age.

Finally, the *Postmodern* worldview first emerged in the 1960s with the advent of computer technology, networking, and globalization and we now associate it with the Information Age.

Now, as we continue this brief overview of worldviews and leadership paradigms, I will introduce the four fundamental leadership paradigms seen across nearly all of the leadership theory literature. This is an important pattern that my colleagues and I at the Integral Institute and the Stagen Leadership Academy discovered that eventually led us to a *Unifying Theory of Leadership that is the foundation of the Universal Leadership Model.*

The Imperial Leadership Paradigm

This is the original and the oldest leadership paradigm. This is the view of leadership that began in the "Bronze Age." In ancient times, leadership was fused with "power." The person with the power was the leader. Think kings, dukes, tribal chiefs, warlords and so on. Many ancient texts such as the Tao Te Ching by Lao Tzu, the Bible (especially the *Old Testament*), and *The Prince* by Machiavelli describe this Imperial Leadership paradigm.

Bookstores are filled with popular titles that are written by authors who subscribe to this Imperial Leadership Paradigm and who are advocates for it. These numerous books would not be so popular if there wasn't a market for them. Stanly Bing is the author of two such popular titles: *What Would Machiavelli Do? The Ends Justify the Meanness and Sun Tzu Was a Sissy: Conquer Your Enemies, Promote Your Friends, and Wage the Real Art of War.* He suggests that Machiavelli would feel at home in today's corporate world. According to Bing, we live in a "vicious, highly competitive workplace environment, and things aren't getting any better." "Jobs are few and far between," he explains, "and people aren't any nicer now than they were when Genghis Khan ran around killing people in unfriendly acquisitions." "Work is war-like; only the mean advance," he advises. "We must expect nastiness. We must be prepared."

Robert Greene, the author of *The 48 Laws of Power and The 50th Law is* another popular advocate of this Imperial Leadership Paradigm. He writes, "Learning the game of power requires a certain way of looking at the world, a shifting of perspective." People like Bing and Greene who adopt the Imperial Leadership Paradigm believe that everyone wants power and everyone is in a constant duplicitous game to gain more power at the expense of others. It is worth noting that Robert Greene draws inspiration from leaders such as: Machiavelli, Bismarck, Catherine the Great, Mao, Kissinger, and others. His book illustrations are drawn from courts of modern and ancient Europe, Africa and Asia, highlighting the popularity that this Imperial Leadership Paradigm has enjoyed throughout human history, and highlights how popular this paradigm still is today.

Trait Theories

Trait Theories, which were largely discredited in the 1980s only to be revitalized in the 90s, are unfortunately still quite common today. Trait theory stems from a very rudimentary understanding of psychology, where the nuances of beliefs, thinking, social and emotional development, and interpersonal skills are all boiled down into "leader traits." Proponents of Trait Theory also lack "context awareness" or "systems thinking" that would reveal the fairly obvious fact that different contexts, different situations (especially different cultures), call for different traits or "qualities" in leaders. Proponents of Trait Theory subscribe to a "one-size-fits all" view of leadership and are burdened by the erroneous assumption that all followers in all contexts look for the same traits (or qualities) in leaders. While it should be obvious to any intelligent person that these assumptions are wrong, many leadership coaches, leadership trainers and leadership training companies still emphasize leadership traits (or qualities as they are often called) with what seems to be no awareness at all of the different contexts in which leaders find themselves or the different cultures, mindsets, needs and preferences of different follower types. They fail to recognize that different cultures and different followers will be looking for very different qualities in leaders; therefore, there is in fact no set of traits that are universally appreciated by all cultures and followers (therefore there is little merit to Trait Theory). People who have this view of leadership also fail to recognize that leadership is fundamentally a set of skills, not a set of traits (or qualities).

Great Man Theory

The "Great Man Theory" is closely related to "Trait Theory" but bears a special emphasis. Put simply, this theory is on the "leaders are born" side of the "Are leaders born or made" debate. The name of this theory reflects its Bronze-Age origins, it is not the "Great Person Theory," but rather, the "Great MAN Theory" precisely because the proponents of this theory saw leaders as always being men (never women). Examples of "great man" traits character traits include integrity, morals, trustworthiness, judgment, charisma, God-faring, and so on.

Charismatic Leadership

Early proponents of Charismatic Leadership theory believed that charisma was an individual character trait that a person either had or didn't. (This is an example of the "Great Man Theory" and is popular with people who gravitate toward "Leadership Character Traits" frameworks). Later advocates of this style who demonstrate more emotional intelligence, social intelligence, or simply a more comprehensive understanding of interpersonal psychology see this phenomenon called charisma as a quality that emerges, at least in part, from the relationship between leader and follower and not a character trait.

Theory X and Theory Y

You will recall that the Theory X vs. Y leadership framework describes Theory X as being characterized by the assumption of the leader / manager that workers need close supervision and lack motivation and must be coerced to do their work and /or managed with a heavy hand.

Autocratic Leadership

Autocratic leadership can be succinctly defined as "The person with the most power leads via command and control." This is sometimes called "imperialistic" leadership which suggests exerting influence through power or force, also sometimes called "Machiavellian leadership." One of the first and most well-known texts that serve as an instruction guide for this approach to leadership is entitled "The Prince" (an instruction guide for new princes and royals) written in the 16th century by Niccolo Machiavelli. This is how many the Imperial Leadership Paradigm sees followers, as people who must be coerced or manipulated to do their bidding. It is fair to say that Autocratic Leadership is very close to being synonymous with the "Imperial Leadership Paradigm." In 2016 and again in 2024 the American voters voted for a textbook Autocratic leader supported by voters who prefer to follow Autocratic leaders and for which this Imperial leadership paradigm is most appealing.

The Traditional Leadership Paradigm

Traditional Leadership Theories are based on "leadership laws" and/or "leader character traits." Leadership "laws" amount to concrete, unchanging rules that should be followed in every situation.

The main difference between the Traditional leadership paradigm, and the Modern paradigm is that the former places an emphasis on either positional authority or perceived "moral authority." Many of these traditional leadership advocates draw their understanding of leadership psychology from traditional religious texts.

A high-profile proponent of this traditional paradigm is leadership expert John Maxwell, who has sold over 24 million books in 50 languages. Inc. Magazine named him the number one authority on leadership in the United States. His most popular book, *The 21 Irrefutable Laws Of Leadership*, has sold over 4 million copies alone and is an excellent example of the traditional leadership paradigm. His work is not based on a modern or postmodern understanding of psychology or organizational behavior. Where does it stem from? In Maxwell's own words, "Everything I know about leadership I learned from reading and studying the Bible." In the following section, I will summarize a few of the most popular traditional paradigm approaches.

Trait Theories and Great Man Theories

I will mention Trait Theories and Great Man theories again in this Traditional Leadership Paradigm section because most people who subscribe to this paradigm also believe in these theories. While these theories first emerged as part of the Imperial Leadership

Paradigm, these are also embraced by the Traditional Leadership Paradigm.

Visionary Leadership

These classic leadership theories emphasize a leader's compelling vision for the future or a leader's charismatic personality to influence followers. This classic leadership style uses a leader's compelling vision for the future to drive organizational change and individual performance. Visionary leaders are considered to have self-confidence and high cognitive capability and use power in different ways depending on the context of a given situation. Since we are giving a nod to the element of time (oldest theories first), think of kings, generals or captains who possessed a unique vision for the future or for a real or figurative "destination" and used this vision to influence followers.

Authority Leadership

Authority leadership can be succinctly defined as "The person with positional authority leads via chain of command". This is a "hierarchical" approach to leadership. Followers are expected to dutifully comply with the established protocols to coordinate efforts to meet requirements prescribed by the authority figure (the leader or the institution). While "authoritarian leadership" is the correct term used by academics and journalists, many people who subscribe to this style of leadership may bristle at being described as "authoritarian" because that term is often used (accurately) to describe "authoritarian regimes" in countries that subscribe to "authoritarian rule." Because of this, we often substitute this term with "Authority Leadership," "Bureaucratic Leadership" "Chain of Command Leadership" or "Rule-Centric" leadership. These are all useful euphemisms (and synonyms) for what academics call authoritarian leadership. It is fair to say that "Authority Leadership" is very close to being synonymous with the "Traditional Leadership Paradigm."

The Modern Leadership Paradigm

As the name implies, the Modern Leadership Paradigm benefits from modern psychology and an industrial or post-industrial view of business management. Think of Tom Peter's "search for excellence" in the 1980s, Peter Drucker's modern management theory, and strategy, and innovation pioneers such as Michael Porter and Clayton Christenson, Harvard Business Review articles, and so on.

The modern paradigm emphasizes how scientific and rational dimensions of organizational life lead to "excellence" and/or "competitive advantage." Leadership theorists who view organizational life through this modern lens have developed theories with names like "Competency Theory," "Game Theory," and "Transactional Leadership Theory."

Theory X and Theory Y

This theory was first articulated in 1957 by leadership theorist James McGregor in his book, *The Human Side of Enterprise.* Simply put, if you believe that your team members dislike their work and have little motivation, then, according to McGregor, you'll likely use a more "authority-centric" style of management. This approach is very "hands-on" and may involve micromanaging people's work to ensure that it gets done properly. McGregor called this Theory X (and reflects the Imperial Leadership Paradigm described previously). On the other hand, if you believe that your people take pride in their work and see it as a challenge, then you will be more likely to adopt a more "participative leadership style." Leaders who use this approach tend to trust their people to take ownership of their work and do it effectively by themselves or with much less supervision. McGregor called this Theory Y. McGregor's "Theory Y" is a close synonym to what we call the "Modern Leadership Paradigm."

Democratic Leadership

Democratic leadership, commonly referred to as "participative leadership," is about letting multiple people participate in the decision-making process. This type of leadership can be seen in a wide range of contexts, from businesses to schools to governments. While the Imperial and Traditional paradigms are *autocratic* or *authoritarian* in nature and do not recognize many rights or privileges of followers, this more recent "democratic" view of organizational life, suggests followers should have some kind of say or vote in organizational matters.

Competency Theory

This theory can be seen as a result of a more "modern take" on Traditional leadership theories. Competency Theory applies more sophisticated psychological frameworks to see that to be effective, leaders must possess a specific set of abilities, competencies, or skills, such as: making difficult decisions, problem-solving, the ability to develop and articulate a compelling vision, and the ability to motivate others. Competency Theories transcend the rudimentary understanding of psychology that is reflected in the Imperial and Traditional Leadership Paradigms. By applying more sophisticated psychological frameworks, these theorists suggest that rather than simply having innate character traits, to be effective, leaders must possess a specific set of competencies (another word for skills). Examples of leadership competencies include: decision making, problem solving, developing a vision, executing that vision, holding others accountable, building effective teams, motivating others, effective communication and so on. Unlike character traits, competencies (behaviors/skills) can be learned.

Strengths-Based Leadership Theory

This theory emphasizes specific competencies that are tied to the positive psychology concept of virtues or "character strengths." This is a modern take on the traditional theories of "character traits." What makes this different is that these strengths are seen as both innate gifts and competencies that can be developed and refined over time with training, practice and experience. This theory heavily emphasizes self-awareness of leaders to know their own strengths so that they can surround themselves with others who have complementary strengths.

Contingency Theory

Fred Fiedler's contingency theory suggests that task- or people-oriented leadership style effectiveness depends on the situation (i.e., structure of work, position power, and relationship). This leadership theory holds that no single style works with all types of people, and rather, the best leadership style depends on the situation and circumstances (including the people being led). This is a very important development in the Modern Leadership Paradigm. Fiedler was one of the first theorists to begin to emphasize the context of leadership (what I often call circumstances). We will expand upon this "context" aware approach as we explain our "integral" leadership methodology.

Path-Goal Theory

This theory emphasizes incentivizing followers to hit milestones toward pre-defined goals. This is essentially Fiedler's "Contingency Theory" with the addition of motivation theory. The idea is that followers are motivated to achieve a goal, and the leader can define the path to that goal and lead them to their desired outcomes. Here again you can see this modern view of seeing leadership as inherently about achieving goals (or hitting targets).

Pragmatic Leadership Theory

This theory emphasizes the practical, "how do we get this done," side of any task, initiative or goal. The primary focus is simply on solving the problem or getting to the end result. It reflects a linear, practical way of thinking about moving an organization forward toward the accomplishment of a goal.

Managerial Grid

As mentioned previously, Robert Blake and Jane Mouton's Managerial Grid is based on two factors: task orientation versus people orientation which when placed on an X-Y grid produces four different approaches to leadership. This reflects modern theorists recognition of different circumstances and different followers (which is largely absent from the Imperial and Traditional views of leadership).

Action-Centered Leadership

Action-centered Leadership Theory is essentially Blake and Mouton's Managerial Grid (task orientation and people orientation) expanded with the notion that effective leaders focus on three dimensions (not two). Those three dimensions are task, team, and individual.

Situational Leadership

Bernard Bass and others have proposed a contingency model (drawn from Contingency Theory) that includes directive, consultative, participative and delegative approaches. Ken Blanchard, perhaps best known as the author of the bestseller "The One Minute Manager," drew inspiration from Bass' framework to create what he called "Situational Leadership Theory" which he popularized in his other best-selling book, "Leadership and the One Minute Manager" in 1985. Strictly speaking, "situational leadership" is a model of management styles and has little if anything to do with leadership. It encourages matching the management style with the preferred working style of subordinates based on a simple X-Y framework, with the two poles of "direction" and "support" producing four behaviors. It is a useful and pragmatic framework for management.

Game Theory

According to Game Theory, people are motivated primarily, if not entirely, by rational behaviour that seeks to maximize how much one can gain from each interaction. This reflects the modern view that human motivation is largely, or exclusively, centered around individual gain. This is a very narrow and limited view of human motivation, yet it is the basis of not only game theory, it is also the basis of modern economic theory. (As we will see in the Postmodern Leadership Paradigm section that follows, later theorists learned that human motivation is much more complex than simply "individual gain.")

Transactional Leadership

Transactional theories, also known as exchange theories, are characterized by a transaction made between the leader and the follower(s) that results in a mutually beneficial relationship. These theories posit that the leader must find a way to align follower behavior with the leader-assigned goal or task. The transactional leadership theorists believe that humans are seeking to maximize pleasurable experiences and to diminish un-pleasurable experiences. This is similar to the assumptions inherent in *Game Theory* which is one popular but very narrow and limited way to try to understand human motivation. Transactional Leadership theories emphasize extrinsic motivation as incentives for desired follower behavior. These theories emphasize vision, goal achievement, and rationally informed paths to success. Leaders work with others to develop a shared vision and intelligent "plan" that leads to the accomplishment of goals and the steady improvement of the organization. This approach to leadership emphasizes vision, goal achievement, and rationally informed paths to success. Leaders work with others to develop a shared vision and intelligent "plan" that leads to a steady improvement of the organization and ultimately to the accomplishment of the organization's or the leader's goals. This leadership paradigm sees the person with the most expertise as the most qualified leader in most circumstances.

The postmodern theorists like Bass, Avolio and others call this approach "transactional" as a way to denigrate it by comparison with their more humanistic approach that they will name "transformational" (discussed later in this chapter under "Postmodern Theories"). While this approach is unpopular with postmodern theorists, it is highly effective and very popular with many corporate cultures. It is fair to use the term "Strategic Leadership" to summarize most of these theories into a single idea. Strategic Leadership is very close to being synonymous with the "Modern Leadership Paradigm."

The Postmodern Leadership Paradigm

If you aren't familiar with the term "postmodern," let me summarize it here. Postmodern philosophy puts a large emphasis on the subjective nature of experience. The postmodern perspective is considered "pluralistic" because it recognizes multiple truths as opposed to one single absolutistic view of truth. Further, it is seen as desirable to have numerous distinct ethnic, religious, or cultural groups present and tolerated in society. The postmodern paradigm is also called "Relativism."

This view suggests that values and beliefs, and the best ways to think and behave, are relative to one's upbringing, culture, and living conditions.

Many leadership books that promote work-life balance, emotionally aware "resonant" leadership, "egalitarian leadership," "inclusive leadership," and "appreciative inquiry" are reflections of this leadership paradigm. Some of the most popular leadership theories that fall under this postmodern paradigm include: *Transformational Leadership, Emergent Leadership, and Adaptive Leadership.*

As contrasted with methods viewed as more "transactional," these so-called transformational leadership approaches are more people-centric and humanistic. They emphasize tapping people's potential through meaning, shared learning, and mutual empowerment. There are many expressions of this Postmodern Leadership Paradigm, all of which seek to inspire followers while drawing on emotional intelligence, social and political sensitivity, transparency, and authenticity and are always in service of "the greater good."

Emergent Leadership Theory

Emergent Leadership Theory holds that leadership emerges from the group because of a desire to serve others. More "adaptive" and "emergent" approaches have become popular in recent years due to their emphasis on helping organizations and individuals in dealing with change and uncertainty, especially in circumstances, with no clear answers, solutions, or reliable best practices. This theory reflects a "systems view" of organizational change. Systems thinking, as it is often called, is a central feature of this Postmodern leadership paradigm.

Self-Managed Teams

This theory assumes that teams are most effective when there is not a single leader in a position of authority, but rather, leadership is best treated as a phenomenon that arises naturally when all members of a team are allowed to share their views and achieve consensus so that everyone is fully "bought in." There are many books, but the two most popular ones on this topic are *The Discipline of Teams* and *The Wisdom of Teams* by Jon Katzenbach and Doug Smith.

Emergent Leadership Theory

This leadership theory posits that leadership is most effective when no group member is appointed or elected to the leadership role but rather, the leadership phenomenon emerges and develops naturally over time as a result of the group's interaction. This approach is very similar to the "self-managed teams" and "collaborative leadership" approaches described above that empowers team members to make decisions outside the traditional structure of a business organization.

Servant Leadership

Robert Greenleaf's approach has variations on the work of Peter Block and many others. The essence of Servant Leadership is that the organizational chart is turned upside down. The CEO and senior leadership are servants of their direct reports, mid-level management serves the people they support, and the customer is at the (now) top of the organizational chart as the ultimate group to serve. It is easy to see how this non-hierarchical (or upside-down hierarchy), people-centric, humanistic, empowerment approach to leadership is very popular with people with a postmodern worldview. While this theory was created by a theorist with a postmodern worldview and is popular with people with postmodern worldviews, this leadership approach is also quite popular with people with a Traditional worldview who are often resonant with the notion that a leader should be a "servant."

Adaptive Leadership

This leadership theory by Ron Heifetz and Marty Linsky has become quite popular in recent years due to its emphasis on helping organizations and individuals in dealing with change and uncertainty, especially in circumstances, with no clear answers, solutions or reliable best practices. This theory reflects a "systems view" of organizational change which is popular with postmodern thinkers.

Transformational Leadership

Building on the work of James MacGregor Burns, professors Bass and Avolio collected, documented and synthesized what they call "transformational approaches" (as contrasted to what they call "transactional methods"). Transformational leadership approaches combine the "Visionary Leadership" and "Charismatic Leadership" discussed previously with a strong humanistic and people-centric style emphasizing themes that are very popular with people with a postmodern worldview. These include: emotional intelligence, psychological safety, and helping people reach their full potential (often called empowerment). Transformational approaches are a lot more people-centric than "transactional" approaches. Rather than primarily focusing on problem solving, targets, outcomes, strategic plans, incentives and winning (as we see with the more transactional approaches), "transformational" approaches emphasize tapping people's potential through meaning, intrinsic motivation, shared learning, and mutual empowerment. It is fair to use the term "Humanistic Leadership" to summarize most of these theories into a single idea. Humanistic Leadership is very close to being synonymous with the "Postmodern Leadership Paradigm."

The Simplicity on the Other Side of Complexity

If you aren't familiar with the term, which you may recall is also the subtitle of ths book, please allow me to briefly explain. The "first simplicity," as it is called, is the simplicity of a beginner approaching a subject with a rudimentary understanding of a practice or a field of study. Once a person spends many years (and thousands of hours) studying and practicing, they come to understand many details and many nuances about it, and they realize it is quite complex. When you consult with most experts in any field (doctors, attorneys, engineers, etc.) you can experience this "complexity." It is said that it takes approximately 10,000 hours to become an "expert" in most complex skills and professions.

But after a person has invested significantly more time than that and has attained a certain "mastery" of the field, the underlying principles that tie together all the myriad facts, perspectives, strategies and techniques are revealed. Someone with this much experience has an embodied, internalized, and intuitive grasp of the essential principles. In this way, things get simplified. But this is not the simplicity of the beginner who has no clue about the details, technical aspects and nuance of the field. This is rather the simplicity on the other side of complexity that is only revealed after many years (and many thousands of hours past the "10,000 hours" of "expertise"). My years of designing and delivering leadership training programs have revealed a "second simplicity." While all of the academic and theoretical underpinnings described above are helpful, as I see it, in practice, this all really boils down to just three things:

1) *The circumstances* (another word for context, which includes the people involved and their leadership needs and preferences),

2) *Leadership skills* (what leaders actually do, in other words the concrete abilities, techniques, and behaviors); and

3) *Leadership styles* that correspond to the major worldviews or value systems of the followers or group.

In my experience, the three pillars that provide the foundation for an any effective approach to leadership will always be *circumstances, skills* and *styles*! I'm not going to mince words here. To put it bluntly, if you are getting advice from well-meaning but ill-informed leadership coaches or trainers whose advice is not grounded in one, two or all three of these pillars, then you are getting what I call "bogus leadership advice."

Circumstances

If we are mature leaders, leaders who are "context aware," then we must always take into account the circumstances (the context) in which you will use your leadership abilities. If we are to be effective in our role as leaders, we must bring some *sensemaking* acuity to the situation to reasonably answer the questions, "What is really happening?" What is important?" and "What is needed?" A central aspect of the circumstances are the people involved. The most important aspect of the people that effective leaders track is their "mindset" and "motivation." In other words, their worldviews which dictate what leadership behaviors they associate with legitimate, credible leadership. The notion of "circumstances" (context), especially the psychology of the people involved will be explored in more depth in subsequent chapters (linked with specific leader skill sets). That brings us to the next pillar, *skills*.

Skills

The stated purpose of this book is to help you increase your leadership ability which is made up of concrete and specific skills. Therefore, I will emphasize the most crucial leadership behaviors, that is, what effective leaders do. This is the domain of technique and skill. There are three "essential leadership abilities" that all effective leadership demonstrate. Parts II, III and IV of this book are organized around these three abilities and the skill sets that these abilities are comprised of. (Books 2-4 in this series go into even more detail on the skill sets, skills, and techniques.)

That brings us to the final pillar, *styles*.

Styles

We will always bear in mind that effective leaders must approach situations and engage in leadership behaviors using one of the four universal leadership styles outlined in this book. These universal leadership styles are quite well-documented in the leadership literature and are also very intuitive because you've been around these styles your whole life. Perhaps they weren't explained in the same clear terms as this book explains them, but they are, as the saying goes, "as old as the hills."

You only need to open your eyes to see them around you every day and every week, in your organization, in your family and friend groups, in the communities you associate with and participate in, and certainly in the news.

In this chapter, I have provided an overview of leadership theory with an emphasis on why most leadership theories and models contradict one another.

We have seen that these models and theories were created predominantly by men (yes men) who were subject to their own *Imperial, Traditional, Modern or Postmodern* worldviews and therefore their theories reflect the assumptions and biases inherent in each worldview (with regard to what people care about, what people are capable of and what motivates people).

By applying integral psychology to the problem, we can now see that leadership approaches (or styles) must be paired with the psychology (especially the worldview) of the followers if the approach is to be well received or even remotely effective.

This chapter offered a whirlwind tour of leadership theory. I introduced some useful lenses with which to study leadership theory, including the *trait, behavioral, styles,* and *circumstances* views. While the complexity of leadership theory can be overwhelming, it is crucial to have a more nuanced understanding of leadership theory in order to benefit from the legitimate insights (however partial and often uncontextualized) these theories offer us.

As we move on to the next chapter, the *Leadership Rosetta Stone* presents a solution to this problem with leadership theory by providing a simple yet powerful framework for understanding how leadership styles actually work with followers with different psychological makeup. The Leadership Rosetta Stone is literally at the "center" of the Universal Leadership Model. It is also the most unique aspect of the model (no other leadership model, at least at the time of this writing, includes it).

CHAPTER 3:
THE LEADERSHIP ROSETTA STONE

The Rosetta Stone is an ancient Egyptian artifact on which. the same information is inscribed in: Egyptian hieroglyphs, Demotic, and Greek. The discovery of the Rosetta Stone allowed researchers to decode the language of Egyptian hieroglyphs for the first time in history.

The phrase "Rosetta Stone" is often used idiomatically to describe any critical key that unlocks something previously difficult (or impossible) to decipher. After reviewing hundreds of leadership texts, including most of the popular books on leadership theory and practice, an unmistakable pattern emerged for me and my research team at The Integral Institute (under the mentorship of Ken Wilber) and the Stagen Leadership Academy. Nearly all "leadership theory" texts and books that claim to explain the "best" way to lead describe the writers' subjective ideas about which leadership tactics work best with followers based on their own assumptions about the world and the people being led. All of the texts that described the authors' opinions about which leadership techniques/approaches work best with followers are based on their assumptions about the world and the people being led.

With rare exceptions, the authors' inherent assumptions about the world and people (and biases for which approaches should be used) lined up with the four "worldviews" I had learned about from Ken Wilber, Jean Gebser, Robert Kegan and the other developmental psychologists I had studied or worked with.

This turned out to be the key to unlocking the Universal Theory of Leadership. When we group the leadership theories, approaches, techniques and tools by the worldview of their advocate, we see that in most cases, those methods do work well for followers who share that worldview. Integral theory provides us with an easy way (if you know what to look for) to identify follower mindsets, or worldviews.

Therefore, if we know a follower's worldview, we will know with a great deal of accuracy which leadership styles and approaches will be most resonant with them, that they will feel drawn to, will trust, willingly follow, and the leader for whom they will happily offer their "discretionary effort

Next, I will first summarize the four most common worldviews most relevant in organizational life in the developed world and briefly introduce the four universal leadership styles and show how you apply them to the three essential leadership abilities and nine leadership core competencies.

The Four Universal Worldviews

In a later section entitled "Values Research," I will provide a detailed description of decades of values and worldviews research that demonstrates that nearly all major theorists (who study values and worldviews) agree that there are four universal worldviews, and nearly all also agree on their common names). For now, I will keep the discussion brief and simply introduce the Four Universal Worldviews that are essential building blocks for our Leadership Rosetta Stone. These four worldviews should be familiar to you by now as I introduced them previously when I explained the four leadership paradigms.

The Imperial Worldview

The Imperial worldview first emerged in society during the time of feudal kingdoms and is roughly equivalent to the Bronze Age and is still very much alive and well today. People with this worldview see the world as made up of "predators and prey", where the strongest and most cunning survive, gain power, and satisfy their wants. They tend to be fiercely independent living by their "own rules" and are disinterested in conforming to many social norms, are driven to break free from limits, achieve their goals, or impose their will. People with this worldview tend to believe the best way to think and behave is "my way." People with an Imperial worldview find the Autocratic leadership style most credible.

The Traditional Worldview

The Traditional worldview initially emerged historically with the monotheistic religious traditions and the Roman Empire, and we see it starting with the Iron Age (and continuing through the Middle Ages.) People with this worldview see the world as an ordered existence under the control of a higher authority and ultimate truth. They tend to see the world in a concrete, literal, and dualistic manner: right vs. wrong, good vs. evil, and so on. They emphasize social stability and "mainstream" morality. People with this worldview tend to believe that there is only one right way to think and behave. People with a Traditional worldview will find the Authority style (also called Bureaucratic) most credible.

The Modern Worldview

The Modern Age emerged during the historical western enlightenment and the dawn of scientific thinking we associate with "The Renaissance" which eventually led to the Industrial Age. People with this worldview tend to believe in the advancement of humankind through the application of the rational mind and its scientific, technological, and medical manifestations. Life is to be met and mastered by finding the best way to act on its limitless opportunities. People with this worldview tend to believe that while there are many valid ways to think and behave, there is always one best way. People with Modern worldview will find the Strategic leadership style most credible.

The Postmodern Worldview

The Postmodern worldview first emerged in the 1960s with the advent of computer technology, networking and globalization and we associate it with the Information Age. People with this worldview believe the world is a diverse web of interrelationships where life forms depend on each other for survival, and there is no single explanatory system (view of reality) that can account for all the phenomena of life; rather there are many truths. People with this worldview tend to believe that there are many valid ways to think and behave but that there is no real way to judge the superiority of one way or another. People with Postmodern worldview will find the Humanistic leadership style most credible.

Now that we've defined the four worldviews, let's look at the four "universal leadership styles" that must be paired with people who share these corresponding worldviews in order for you to be viewed as a credible leader by your followers.

The Four Universal Leadership Styles

To aid in the learning process, I will first provide a "flyover" with the four very brief definitions and descriptions of the four universal leadership styles that provide a hub that the Universal Leadership Model spins around. These will already be familiar to you because they track perfectly with the four "Leadership Paradigms" (that were created by leadership theorists who are subject to one of the four universal worldviews) that I introduced in the last chapter.

1) *Autocratic Leadership:* The person with the most power leads via command and control. In short, this leadership style is based on power and control. Of course, this style goes by many names, but for simplicity's sake, we are choosing one.

2) *Authority Leadership:* The person with positional authority leads via chain of command. In short, this leadership style is based on rules and compliance. Again, this style goes by many names, but for simplicity's sake, we are choosing this one.

3) *Strategic Leadership:* The person with the most expertise leads via strategic planning and tangible incentives. In short, this leadership style is based on expertise and winning. Once again, this style goes by many names, but for simplicity's sake, we are choosing this one.

4) *Humanistic Leadership:* Leadership is not vested in any one person; rather, it emerges from the collective via consensus in the service of the greater good. In short, this leadership style is based on equality and consensus. Finally, this style goes by many other names, but we will us this one.

Now that you have a basic idea of what these four styles are, I will elaborate on the above simple definitions and add a a little more detailed description of each style. A quick comment about a convention I frequently use when teaching, or explaining something, in the case of this "conversation" we are having about the Universal Leadership Model. As the old saying goes, "repetition is the mother of skill." When learning a new model or framework (or technique or practice), it is helpful to go over it multiple times iteratively, and after one layer of understanding is internalized, then add another layer with some additional nuance. You may notice that method being used throughout this book (and my other books). So, in that spirit, let's do another pass across the four styles and add the next layer of nuance.

Autocratic Leadership

Simple definition: The person with the most power leads via command and control.

Approach: This style utilizes a unilateral approach. The leader imposes their will through reputation, fear and respect, tightly control information and choices, reward compliance and punish disloyalty.

Appreciated by: This style is appreciated by people with predominantly Imperial worldviews who respect dominance and aggression, and who prefer to follow leaders who are perceived as being the strongest, toughest, and most dominant and who will be able to protect them from (or defeat) their enemies.

Authority Leadership

This is also known as "Bureaucratic Leadership" and "chain of command" leadership.

Simple definition: The person with positional authority leads via chain of command.

Approach: This style utilizes a hierarchical approach. The leader leverages their position (or title) to compel followers to comply with established rules (and protocols) and to coordinate efforts to meet requirements prescribed by authority.

Appreciated by: People with Traditional worldviews who value honor, service, loyalty, and conformity, and share traditional beliefs and a willingness to sacrifice now for future rewards... and who prefer to follow leaders who are perceived as having positional and/or moral authority

Strategic Leadership

This is also known as "Expert Leadership." Some academics who are strongly biased toward the next style (Humanistic) will refer to this style as "Transactional leadership."

Simple definition: The person with the most expertise leads via strategic planning and tangible incentives.

Approach: This style utilizes a transactional approach. Leaders leverage tangible incentives (often financial) to motivate individuals and teams to execute strategic plans in order to achieve goals (which often includes outperforming peers or competitors).

Appreciated by: People with a Modern worldview who seek opportunities to advance toward their individual goals and who prefer to follow leaders who are perceived as having the most expertise and ability to achieve goals.

Humanistic Leadership

This is also known as "Transformational Leadership," "Collaborative leadership," and "Self-Managed Teams" (the members lead themselves).

Simple definition: Leadership is not vested in any one person; rather, it emerges from the collective via dialog and consensus in the service of "the greater good."

Approach: This style utilizes a transformational approach. Leaders invite people's feelings and intuition via dialog to arrive at a consensus, then work collaboratively toward common goals.

Appreciated by: People with a Postmodern worldview who abhor hierarchy and emphasize diversity, equality, inclusivity, connection, and authenticity, and who strongly prefer to follow leaders who are perceived as being aware, sensitive to the well-being of others, who strive for consensus, and who always treat others as equals.

In the next section, I will quickly review the correct pairings of leadership styles with follower worldviews, before we move on to the inherent leadership responsibilities and the nine leadership core competencies that are essential elements in our Universal Leadership Model.

Pairing Leadership Styles with Follower Worldviews

Followers with an *Imperial* worldview will find Autocratic leadership credible. If you use any of the other three styles with a person with an Imperial worldview, you run the risk of undermining your credibility.

People with a *Traditional* worldview will find Authority leadership credible. Again, if you use any of the other three styles with a person with a Traditional worldview, you run the risk of undermining your credibility because they won't see you as a legitimate leader (according to what they look for in a leader).

People with a *Modern* worldview will find Strategic leadership credible. Again, if you use any of the other three styles with a person with a Modern worldview, you run the risk of undermining your credibility as you don't exhibit the qualities (and the approaches) that they associate with credible leaders and competent leadership.

People with a *Postmodern* worldview will find Humanistic leadership credible. Again, if you use any of the other three styles with a person with a Postmodern worldview, you run the risk of undermining your credibility by appearing clueless or even foolish.

Later in chapter 7, I will even describe exactly what people with a postmodern worldview think of leaders who are using the other three types of leadership (and will do the same for the other three worldviews).

The Theorists Are Also Subject to Their Worldviews

By now you are starting to recognize the pattern that my mentor Ken Wilber first pointed out to me. He called this broadbrush patterns "orienting generalizations" and used them to build "Integral Theory." Naturally different researchers in different contexts (and cultures) will use different names and there will be some variation in their descriptions, but if you possess the requisite cognitive complexity and the capacity for abstract thinking, you can zoom out and as Peter Drucker famously advised, "Get up in your psychological helicopter," and from this larger perspective, the shapes of these "orienting generalizations quickly come into view. Think of the "longitude and latitude lines" on a map, or the conventions of North, South, East and West. Those orienting generalizations are incredible useful, and in truth, they are essential for an accurate map. But those broadbrush generalizations are not substitutes for the more detailed descriptions of a specific town on the map, much less the culture and the local environment that is merely implied by the map. If you fixate on the tiny details, you can't "see the forest for the trees" as the well-known aphorism suggests.

I'm hopeful that the value of Wilber's "orienting generalizations" is making good sense to you. Naturally, a "universal" model or framework for the noble art of leadership would be impossible without them. As I have mentioned, the four universal worldviews track perfectly with the four widely acknowledged "paradigms of leadership" put forth by the different experts. The theorists who put forth leadership theories are often subject to their own worldview biases. The advocates of the different approaches (or styles of leadership as I call them) can be seen clearly to hold these different worldviews. In most cases their bias is unconscious, and they do not admit or acknowledge the existence of the other three worldviews. And they certainly don't agree that the other leadership paradigms (other than the one they are biased towards) holds any merit at all.

This is obviously absurd and reflects the fact that they are ignoring the "context" dimension of leadership. Perhaps most embarrassing of all, many so-called leadership experts and leadership training programs seem to leave out followers altogether! Most of the most respected leadership authorities have overlooked this pattern that the follower's mindset (worldview) determines, in large part, which "leadership paradigm" will offer the most utility in that context. Chapter 7 of this book is devoted to matching the right leadership styles with the right follower worldviews. For now, let's explore universal "leadership responsibilities."

This chapter has introduced you to The Leadership Rosetta Stone. This is an important topic that warrants a much longer treatment.

If this interests you, see my book, *The Leadership Rosetta Stone: Discover Which Leadership Approaches Will Work With Which People and Circumstances and Which Approaches Will Be Disastrous Failures with Which People and Circumstances.*

CHAPTER 4: LEADERSHIP ABILITIES AND COMPETENCIES

In this chapter, we will explore the three essential leadership abilities and the core competencies that underpin them. These competencies, or skill sets, are integral to how leaders fulfill their inherent responsibilities. By examining the critical activities leaders perform, we can clearly identify their responsibilities, the abilities they rely on to meet those responsibilities, and the specific skill sets they develop to succeed. These activities can be grouped into three distinct categories per dimension, creating a total of nine skill sets that form the foundation of effective leadership. These skill sets encompass a rich array of concepts, principles, best practices, tools, and techniques, which are central to this leadership series. In the chapter that follows this one, "Building a Universal Model of Leadership," these skill sets will be presented as the outermost layer of the model, representing its most detailed dimension. Before delving into the visual structure of the model, it is essential to establish a clear understanding of these skill sets, beginning with leadership responsibilities.

Inherent Leadership Responsibilities

As stated in the introduction, three inherent leadership responsibilities have always been and will always be central to leadership. These responsibilities go by many different names (that reflect different organizational cultures and contexts), but for our purposes here, I will use language that should be familiar to most readers. Using the accelerated learning convention of deliberate and nuanced repetition, we will take this opportunity to revisit some building blocks I introduced earlier.

1. Responsibility for "Planning"

Leaders are responsible for what we think of and are commonly referred to as planning or direction, setting leaders, analyzing organizational opportunities and challenges, setting vision, aligning stakeholders, and crafting winning strategic plans.

Have you ever felt like your organization is spinning its wheels—busy, but not making real progress? Or maybe you're solving problems, only to realize they weren't the right problems to solve? If so, you're not alone. This is where the Planning dimension of leadership comes into play, and it's the foundation of everything we achieve as leaders.

Let's talk about what the Planning dimension really means. At its core, Planning is about creating clarity and focus. It's about defining where we're going as an organization, understanding the landscape we're operating in, and ensuring everyone is aligned and committed to a shared vision. Planning includes crafting a purpose, vision, and values, evaluating challenges and opportunities, and prioritizing the highest-leverage objectives. And here's the kicker—none of this happens in isolation. Engaging stakeholders and earning their commitment is just as important as the strategies and plans we create.

Now, let me ask you a few questions to reflect on your organization:

- How do you make sense of your current environment to identify the best solutions for your challenges and opportunities?
- Is your organization's vision clear enough to inspire alignment and commitment from every key stakeholder?
- And when it comes to making decisions, is your process fast and effective, or does it sometimes feel bogged down?

These questions aren't just theoretical—they're critical for diagnosing where your organization stands and what might need to change.

Let's be real for a moment. Planning isn't always easy. Here are some of the most common frustrations leaders face in this dimension:

- Misinterpreting what the organization really needs—and solving the *wrong* problems.
- Missing opportunities because we're too focused on the wrong priorities.
- Struggling with slow or ineffective decision-making processes.
- Dealing with misalignment or lack of commitment to strategies from leadership teams.

And to top it all off, we're navigating environments filled with uncertainty, complexity, and rapid change. Sound familiar? If you've experienced any of these, you're not alone. The good news? There are proven ways to address these challenges.

One of the most effective ways to assess your organization's planning capabilities is to evaluate where you stand using benchmarks.

- If your organization is in the lower range of proficiency in this ability, planning might feel reactive. There's little clarity around vision, few written plans, and low stakeholder commitment.
- In the intermediate range of proficiency in this ability, you've made progress. You have plans, and your vision is articulated, but you might struggle with deeper stakeholder buy-in or dynamic connections between strategies and execution.
- In the higher range of proficiency in this ability, planning feels like a well-oiled machine. Vision, strategy, and stakeholder commitment are seamlessly integrated. Your organization is not just reacting—it's proactively shaping its future.

Where would you place your organization on this spectrum? And more importantly, where do you *want* it to be?"

Let's pivot and turn our focus to the next dimension of leadership.

2. Responsibility for "Teaming"

Leaders are responsible for what we think of as teaming and relationships, and this dimension is also sometimes referred to as culture. Leaders are expected to set employees up for success, give direction and feedback effectively, know how to listen, dialogue and collaborate with their employees and peers, and be able to keep individuals engaged and motivated and also keep morale high on teams.

Have you ever worked with a team where things just *clicked*? Communication was seamless, everyone was motivated, and the culture felt supportive and energized. Now, imagine the opposite— a team where misunderstandings, disengagement, and low morale drag everything down. The difference isn't luck—it's leadership in the Teaming dimension. Let's explore how to elevate your teamwork and culture to drive success.

The Teaming dimension of leadership is all about setting your people up for success by creating the right environment. It's about fostering a healthy culture, encouraging open communication, and building trust. Great teaming means your people aren't just working *together*—they're thriving as a team. This involves mastering interpersonal skills like listening, giving feedback, and resolving conflicts, as well as motivating a diverse workforce and keeping everyone engaged and aligned with your organization's mission.

Let's pause for a moment and reflect:

- Is your team structured and supported in a way that truly sets people up for success?
- How effective is your team's communication? Are misunderstandings and assumptions slowing you down?
- What strategies are you using to keep your people engaged and motivated—especially when your workforce is diverse, with different needs and drivers?

Take a moment to think about these questions because answering them honestly can help you pinpoint where your team is thriving and where there's room for growth."

Teaming isn't always easy, and many leaders struggle with challenges like these:

- Guarded or defensive communication that creates misunderstandings.
- Personality clashes, unresolved conflicts, or strained relationships between team members.
- Disengaged or unmotivated employees, leading to low morale and poor performance.
- A lack of feedback—or feedback that isn't delivered effectively.

- Issues with trust, diversity, and inclusion that can erode a team's cohesion.

Sound familiar? If you've faced any of these frustrations, you're not alone. These challenges are common—but they're also solvable.

Now, let's reimagine what's possible:

- Your team operates in an environment of trust, where communication is open, honest, and effective.
- New team members are set up for success from day one, and everyone feels supported and valued.
- Conflict is handled constructively, and misunderstandings are minimized.
- Feedback flows naturally—positive and constructive—and keeps your team learning and motivated.
- Morale is high, and team members are engaged and enthusiastic about their work.

This isn't just wishful thinking—it's achievable when we focus on the right strategies to elevate teamwork and culture.

One of the best ways to understand your team's strengths and areas for improvement is by using benchmarks to assess where you are:

- At the lower range of proficiency in this ability, teams struggle with communication, engagement, and trust. Motivation is low, and it's unclear how to build a culture that supports high performance.
- At the intermediate range of proficiency in this ability, teams have decent trust and teamwork, but communication can still feel strained, and engagement isn't consistent across the board. There's a solid foundation, but room to grow.

- At the higher range of proficiency in this ability, communication, culture, and collaboration are strengths. Team members are motivated, engaged, and supported, and feedback and dialog flow effortlessly.

Where does your team fall? And what would it take to move closer to the higher range?

3. Responsibility for "Executing"

Leaders are also responsible for what we think of as "executing" or "implementing." Leaders must identify and close employee performance gaps, achieve high accountability and productivity in their organization, and consistently bring projects successfully across the finish line on time and on budget.

Have you ever worked with a team that just couldn't seem to execute effectively? Deadlines are missed, priorities are unclear, and everyone feels stretched too thin. It's frustrating—and it holds the entire organization back. But here's the thing: great execution isn't about working harder; it's about working smarter. Let's dive into how leaders can master the *Executing* dimension of leadership to drive results and achieve shared goals.

The Executing dimension is where leadership turns plans into results. It's about setting clear roles and responsibilities, identifying performance gaps, and using the right tools to coordinate people, projects, and priorities.
When leaders excel at execution, they don't just manage tasks—they create a culture of accountability, productivity, and focus. And this is especially critical in today's fast-paced, often remote, and distraction-filled work environments.

Let's reflect for a moment:
- How well does your team follow through on commitments? Are performance gaps addressed quickly and effectively?
- Are your feedback and performance reviews driving improvement, or do they feel like a checkbox exercise?
- When it comes to project management, are your processes helping you hit milestones—or are you missing deadlines because of unclear expectations and poor coordination?
- Finally, is your team productive, focused, and organized—even when competing priorities threaten to overwhelm them?

These questions get to the heart of what great execution looks like—and what might be holding your team back."

Execution doesn't happen without effort, and many leaders face frustrations like these:
- A lack of follow-through or accountability across individuals and teams.
- Feeling understaffed and under-resourced yet needing to achieve more with less.
- Unclear expectations that leave employees confused about their roles and responsibilities.
- Ineffective delegation that doesn't produce the desired results.
- Managers and team members feeling overwhelmed by competing priorities and unrealistic workloads.
- Missed deadlines and milestones due to poor project planning and coordination.

Sound familiar? These frustrations are real, but they don't have to be permanent.

Now, imagine this instead:

- Every team member understands their role and what's expected of them.
- Struggling employees receive support to close performance gaps, and accountability is part of the team's culture.
- Projects are planned and managed with clarity, ensuring objectives, timelines, and workstreams are well-coordinated.
- Meetings are purposeful, productive, and drive action—not frustration.
- Time management practices keep everyone focused and efficient, even in complex or high-pressure environments.

This is the power of mastering execution—it turns frustration into momentum and drives results consistently."

Where does your team stand when it comes to execution? Let's break it down with some benchmarks:

- At the lower range of proficiency in this ability, teams often struggle with accountability, time management, and project planning. Performance gaps go unaddressed, and productivity feels inconsistent at best.
- At the intermediate range of proficiency in this ability, teams have started building execution skills. Some members use project management tools and strong productivity practices, but adoption is inconsistent. Accountability conversations happen, but they're often uncomfortable or infrequent.
- At the higher range of proficiency in this ability, execution is a strength. Roles and responsibilities are clear, accountability is part of the culture, and project planning tools are widely used. Teams are focused, efficient, and rarely miss milestones.

Where does your team fall? And what would it take to reach the higher range?"

These three inherent leadership responsibilities (planning, teaming, executing) are featured centrally in our universal leadership model. In fact, as you will see shortly, they take up the most physical space in the model illustration to represent how important "what leaders do" is as it relates to this technical and complex skill called leadership. I will lay out the model graphically in Chapter 5 when I pull all these crucial elements of a complete system of leadership together in the Universal Leadership Model.

But before I do that, there is one more essential element that will be helpful for me to explain first: the nine "core competencies" of effective leaders.

Each of the three "essential abilities" we just discussed (planning, teaming, executing) are made of three skill sets or competencies (for a total of nine). These can also be thought of as the "core practices" of competent leadership.

We will go through the three essential abilities one at a time, starting with planning.

The Three Planning Competencies

Sensemaking

Competent leaders assess the organizational landscape, both external and internal, to determine what is happening, what is important for the team and the organization, and what the leader and organization must do to succeed.

Strategic Alignment

Leaders must set the vision and direction, establish the why (purpose), and clarify the values (the how) of the organization, and then they must also align interests of stakeholders and get buy-in and get commitment to organizational objectives. You could also call this core competency "vision" or "strategic alignment."

Organizational Steering

As a leader, you are responsible for steering the organization. This involves setting goals, crafting winning strategies, and building out adaptable, ever-evolving strategic plans to reliably achieve the objectives each year and each quarter. You could also call this core competency "strategic thinking" or "strategic planning."

The Three Teaming Competencies

Creating the Container

People and teams with different mindsets require different structures and cultures to be effective at various stages of the team's development over time. Effective leaders create a deliberate container and set people up for success. This includes equipping them with the training tools and support they need to be successful.

Communication

Relationships are central to teamwork and communication is key. Competent leaders, manage misunderstandings and conflict, frame and give effective feedback, and use appropriate modes of communication and collaboration.

Motivation

One of the more difficult things leaders are expected to do is to keep individuals engaged and maintain high morale on teams. This requires a keen understanding of mindsets, values, needs, and intrinsic drives.

The Three Executing Competencies

Finally, we will look closely at the three core competencies seen in the execution dimension.

Performance Management

It's the leader's responsibility to identify and close performance gaps with any individuals on their teams. Effective leaders also make expectations explicit, delegate effectively and hold people and teams accountable.

Implementation

Leaders are responsible for ensuring that the work to be done is planned out (workstreams, tasks) and coordinating team schedules (timelines) so that all projects can be predictably successful each quarter and each month on time and on budget.

Productivity

Leaders are responsible for utilizing the resources they have efficiently and productively. The leader must keep the team organized, focused, and efficient. This is the world of calendars, task lists, effective meetings, and so on.

Now I have introduced the nine "competencies" that all effectie leaders share (by any name). Prior to that I introduced the three inherent leadership responsibilities, and before that we reviewed four follower worldviews and the four approaches or "styles" that they find legitimate and credible (based on the assumptions, values, beliefs, needs and preferences inherent in their worldview).

Now, the moment that you have been waiting for... drum roll please... we are ready to assemble the Universal Leadership Model!

CHAPTER 5: BUILDING A UNIVERSAL MODEL OF LEADERSHIP

When we combine the "Leadership Rosetta Stone" which clearly articulates four distinct approaches to leadership with the "Inherent Leadership Responsibilities" and the nine "Leadership Core Competencies" you have a model of leadership that will be universally applicable

All leaders everywhere, regardless of context, share these three inherent responsibilities. Of course, they may go by different names according to different cultures (and when viewed and expressed by people who subscribe to the four leadership paradigms).

All leaders everywhere fulfill their three inherent responsibilities by engaging in the activities we see under each of the nine leadership skill sets (also called "core competencies."

Naturally, the activities, techniques, and skills have different names, but the work of leadership is universal, as are the skills leaders require to be effective. What is different from culture to culture and leader to leader is the "approach" or the "style" with which they undertake these activities. A leader can engage the activities associated with each skill set using any of the four universal leadership styles: *Autocratic, Authority, Strategic,* and *Humanistic.* As you will see, this is situated literally at the "center" of the model.

In this section, we will assemble the "Universal Leadership Model" from the components we have already introduced: 1) *The Leadership Rosetta Stone, 2) Inherent Leadership Responsibilities* and *3) Leadership Core Competencies.*

For clarity's sake, I will bring one in at a time, illustrate and describe each component, and then combine them as we assemble our Universal Leadership Model in a step-by-step fashion

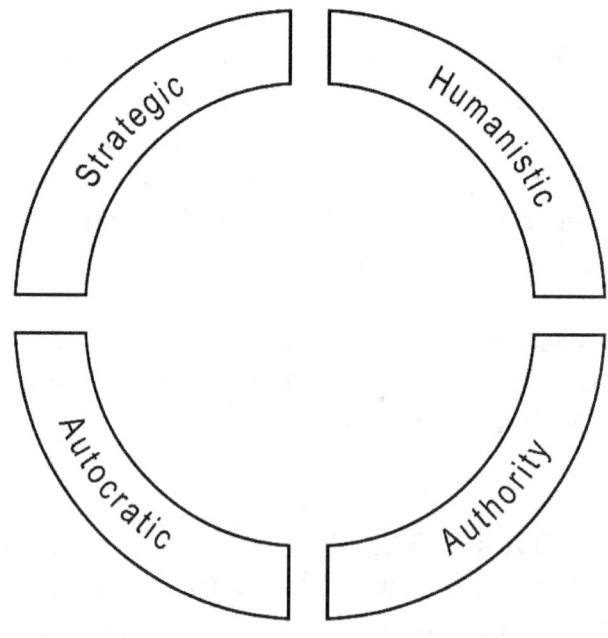

First, recall that the Leadership Rosetta Stone revealed the four our universal leadership styles: *Strategic, Humanistic, Authority*, and *Autocratic*.

Next, the *Leadership Rosetta Stone* revealed the four predominant worldviews

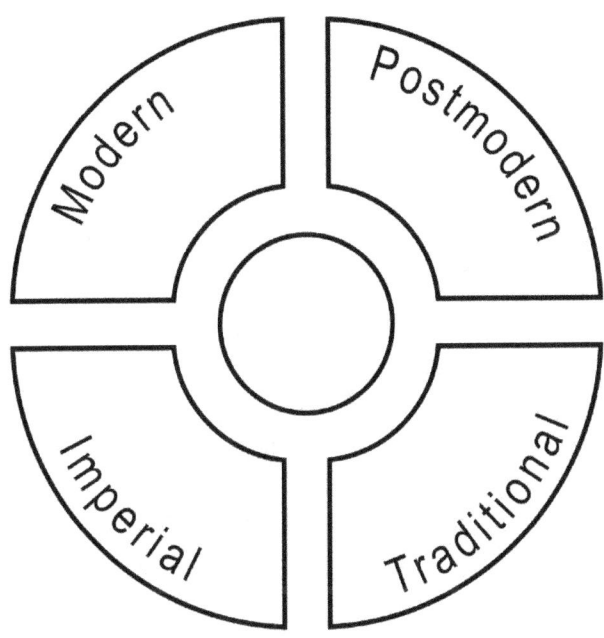

And we learned that each worldview has a specific definition of legitimate leadership and is looking for very different things in people who they view as credible leaders; therefore, to be effective, the correct leadership style must be paired with the follower's worldview.

When we bring the styles together with the worldviews, we can illustrate it like this.

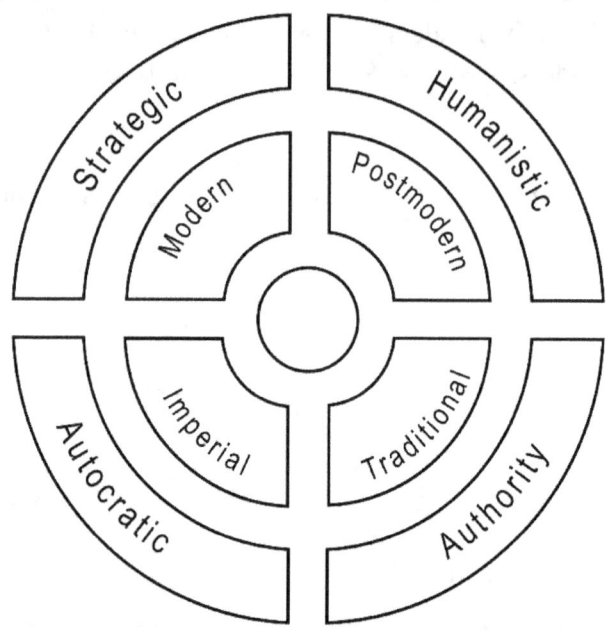

In this illustration, we can see that the correct leadership style is paired with the worldview of the follower (according to the style of leadership that follower will view as credible and legitimate). I devote a whole chapter to this crucial principle of matching the correct leadership style with the follower's worldview.

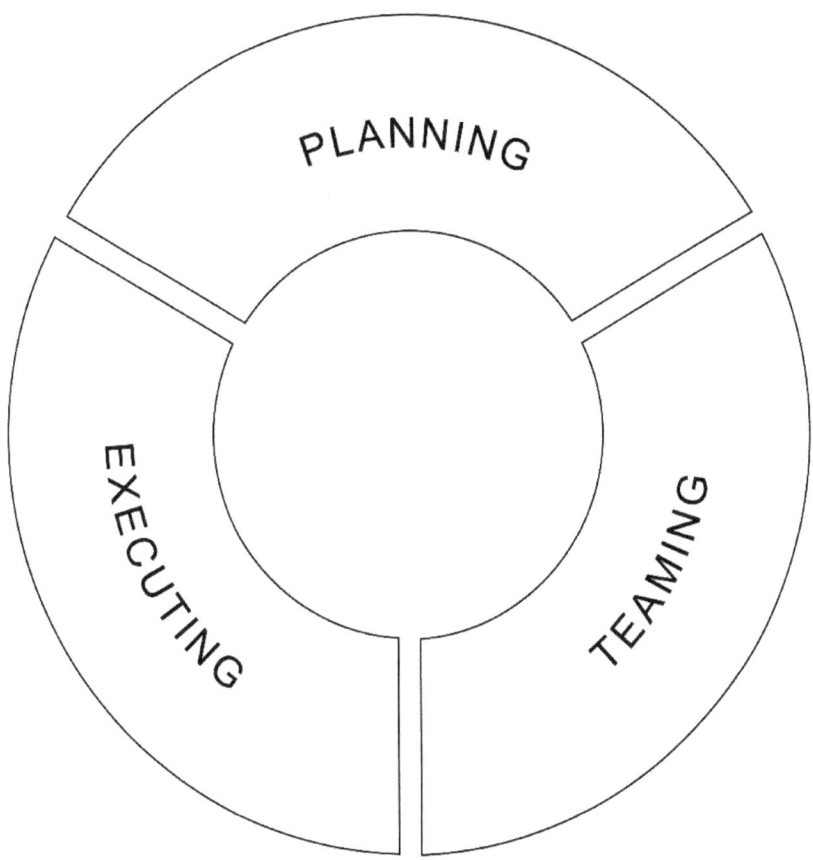

Next, you'll recall that there are three "Inherent Leadership Responsibilities," which correspond to the three "Essential Abilities" that all leaders must have in order to be considered competent and adequately well-rounded.

Generally speaking, using common terms, these are usually referred to as *Planning, Teaming and Executing*. We can use different terms for those fundamental responsibilities and abilities for different audiences and different contexts.

When you take into account the leadership style, you can see that different types of leaders will take a different approach, that is, use a different style as they fulfill these responsibilities. Put another way, all leaders demonstrate three essential abilities, but they use different styles.

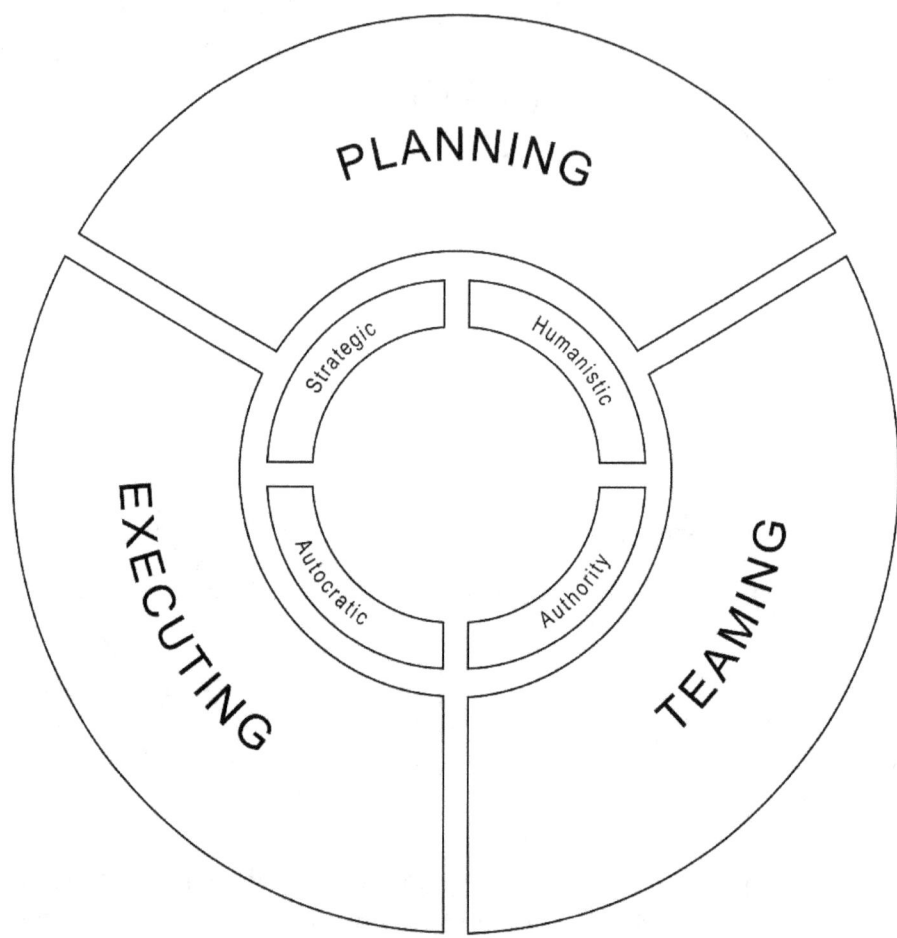

For example, one leader may use a "Humanistic" approach to *planning, teaming* and *executing*. Another leader may use an "Autocratic" approach, another a "Strategic" approach and another a "Authority" approach.

This fact is reflected in our illustration with the four different styles pictured inside the three responsibilities. While this is a static illustration, you might want to imagine the center circle (with the leadership styles) spinning around so that different styles can be deployed with different areas of responsibilities.

Sadly, some leaders lack any versatility at all, and always use their native style (example: Strategic) with all followers. The result of only using one style is that it is only resonant with those followers who have that corresponding worldview (values and beliefs). For the other estimated 25- 75% of the people in typical diverse organizations (who have a different worldview), that leader's style comes across as ineffective, out of touch, lame, not trustworthy, clueless or even foolish. Imagine how ridiculous the positional, "parental," authority style comes across to postmodern followers who despise hierarchy and believe that legitimate leaders always treat everyone as equals. Get it?

Versatile leaders (this includes all leaders who have had the benefit of my Integral Leadership training) develop much-needed capacity to switch their style up and emphasize different leadership styles with different people and circumstances, as the situation warrants.

For example, they can adopt a more Strategic style with their modern worldview, goal-oriented, success- driven followers, and then they lean on a more Humanistic style with their postmodern worldview, progressive followers who expect to be treated as an equal (and expect their feelings and perspectives to be respected and taken into account on all major organizational decisions). And that same versatile leader will adopt a more "hierarchical" Authority approach with their Traditional worldview followers who see legitimate leaders as using their positional authority to enforce rules and compliance.

Next, you will recall that for each of the inherent leadership responsibilities, that leaders engage a variety of practices, activities, skill sets and/or "competencies" to fulfill their responsibilities. In our pragmatic framework, we describe three core competencies (or simply "skill sets") for each of the three responsibilities (3 skill sets x 3 responsibilities = 9 total skill sets).

This next simplified illustration shows the three essential abilities (in the middle area) along with the nine skill sets around the outer ring).

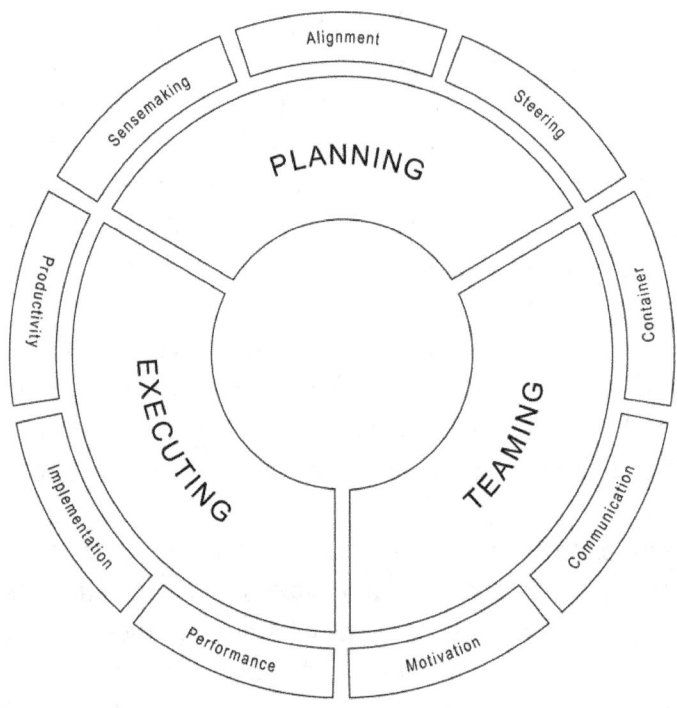

The above illustration shows the three essential abilities along with the nine "leadership core competencies" or "skill sets."

Put another way, these nine skill sets can be thought of as "buckets of activities" that leaders engage in to fulfill their three inherent leadership responsibilities.

Each of these nine skill sets consists of about half a dozen techniques (behaviors, not concepts).

Next, we will want to bring the four leadership styles and four follower worldviews back into our illustration. This way, our illustration reflects that leaders can engage their three "essential abilities" (*planning, teaming and executing*) in the middle of the diagram, along with their corresponding (3x3) skill sets along the outer ring using any of these leadership styles, and those styles should be paired up correctly based on the followers being led.

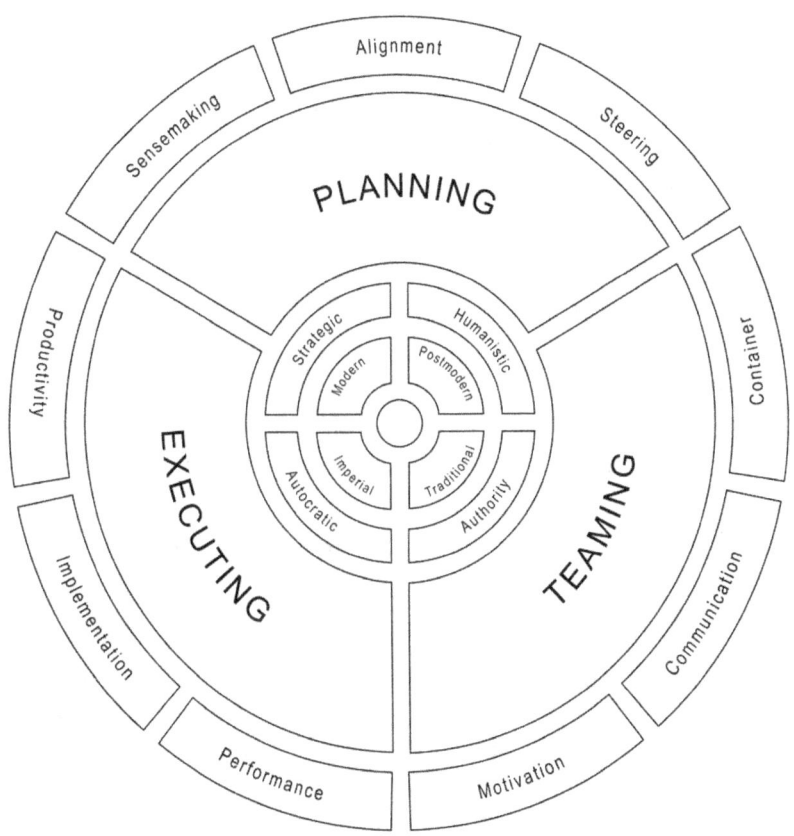

Like so. Now, this version of the model visually suggests that for each ability (middle section) and for each of the nine skill sets (outer section), there are four different styles to draw upon.

There is, for example, a "authority" based way of holding people accountable for their job performance and a "strategic" way of holding people accountable for their performance. There is an "autocratic" approach to creating the team "container" and there is a "humanistic" approach to creating a container (and they are as different as night and day). Similarly, there is a "humanistic" way to approach alignment around vision, for example, and there is a "strategic" way to approach coming up with the vision and aligning people around it. As a final example, there is an autocratic way to motivate people and teams, a authoritarian way, and of course a more humanistic way.

Once you have experience working with this framework, you will realize it provides a nearly unlimited amount of versatility to the art and science of leadership. Mastering this approach will enable you to be an effective leader with a diverse population of followers. Eventually you will be able to influence, motivate, inspire and guide just about anyone, regardless of their worldview.

At first, this notion of leading with the requisite versatility of shifting from "Strategic" style to the "Humanistic" or "Authority" style appears difficult. Yet, my 22 years of teaching leaders to do this shows that it is actually easier than it looks. It just takes instruction from someone who knows this framework, and a lot of practice.

Simply put, to expand your versatility, you will need to select the next style you want to master, find a role model to emulate (and/or read my other books or take one of my many courses), and then practice the new style until it feels natural.

Here is a slightly longer instruction on how to do this.

Recall that the three most common worldviews in most organizations are *Traditional, Modern* and *Postmodern*. The good news is you already have one style down, I call that one your "native style." It is likely either Strategic or Humanistic (that pairs with the Modern and Postmodern follower worldviews respectively). If your role models were highly traditional, then maybe your native style is Authority (also called Bureaucratic).

That hierarchical style must only be used with followers with Traditional worldviews. (The other types of followers will find that "parental" approach quite off-putting, especially the postmodern types who hate hierarchy and expect legitimate leaders to treat everyone as an equal.)

Now, after you identify your "native" style, reflect on your team, organization and the followers you interact with the most.

In this example, I will assume your native style is Strategic. Well, you certainly have all the followers in your organization who have a Modern worldview covered.

What's the next largest group?

Is it Postmodern? If you work in tech or with a younger workforce (millennials and Gen Z) then you probably work with a lot of followers with the postmodern worldview. So then the "Humanistic" style is the one you want to master next!

The best way to learn that style (besides taking one of my courses) is to identify other leaders in your organization, and teachers and mentors, who are "fluent in that values dialect" and who either use the Humanistic style natively or have mastered it through practice.

Study them, notice how they always say "we" and almost never say "I". Notice how they let everyone else speak first before they speak. (Autocratic and Authority leaders would never do that.) Pay attention to how these "Humanistic" leaders demonstrate respect for everyone's perspective, how they treat everyone as their equal, and how they strive for consensus. Also notice the way that they hold people accountable, delegate, give feedback, motivate, handle group decisions and just about every other leader responsibility and activity is undertaken in a slightly different way than you do (contrasting the Humanistic style with the Strategic style in this hypothetical example).

The details of their Humanistic style should be obvious now that I have given you the "leadership styles cheat codes" in the form of my Leadership Rosetta Stone). The answers are all around you, you just needed to know what to look for. And now you know exactly what to look for.

Before we move on, there are still two more elements to represent in the "Universal Leadership Model" that we have started to assemble.

Can you guess what is still missing in our illustration so far?

We have covered followers, leadership styles, leadership responsibilities and leadership skills.

One hint is to recall the element that our leadership industry whistleblowers from Harvard and Stanford (Keller and Pfeffer) point out that is so often ignored.

Perhaps you guessed it.

Organizational context (or what I also call circumstances). Whether or not a given leader and their style (or approach) will be effective is largely a function of the context (the circumstances). As history has shown us repeatedly, an incompetent, failed, discredited leader in one context will be heralded as a brilliant successful leader in a different context (with a different audience). Two examples come to mind: Winston Churchill and Donald Trump. (Barbara Kellerman wrote an excellent book on the latter, entitled *The Enablers: How Team Trump Flunked the Pandemic and Failed America.*)

In the below visual we can see the leader (represented by small circle in the middle) and the organizational context (outer circle).

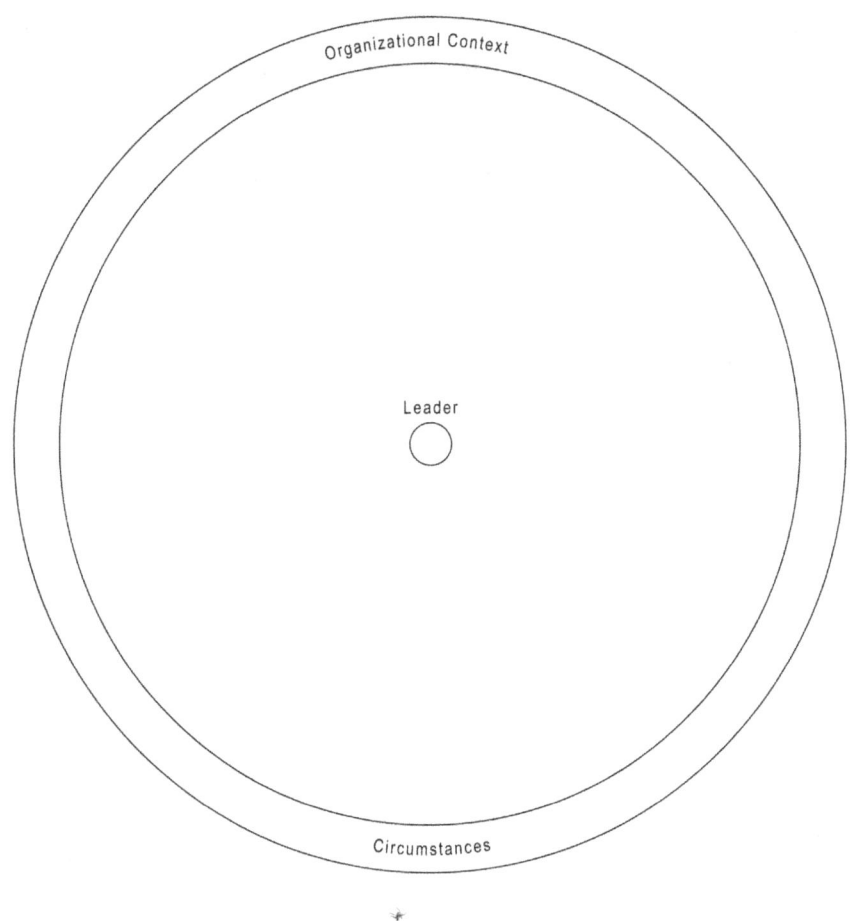

To be effective, a leader must first and foremost be able to make sense out of their circumstances. In our sensemaking trainings (and in other books), we invite leaders to ask the following questions: "What is really happening? What is important? What is needed?" And, "What is the most helpful action I can take?" The next most important thing for a leader to understand after understanding the organizational context (the circumstances), is who are the followers (or persons) that they wish to influence (or lead)? So, the next logical piece of the Universal Leadership Model to bring back in will be the "followers" and we need to especially take into account their psychological makeup represented by their worldview because this dictates what kind of leadership they will view as legitimate and credible and will want to voluntarily follow.

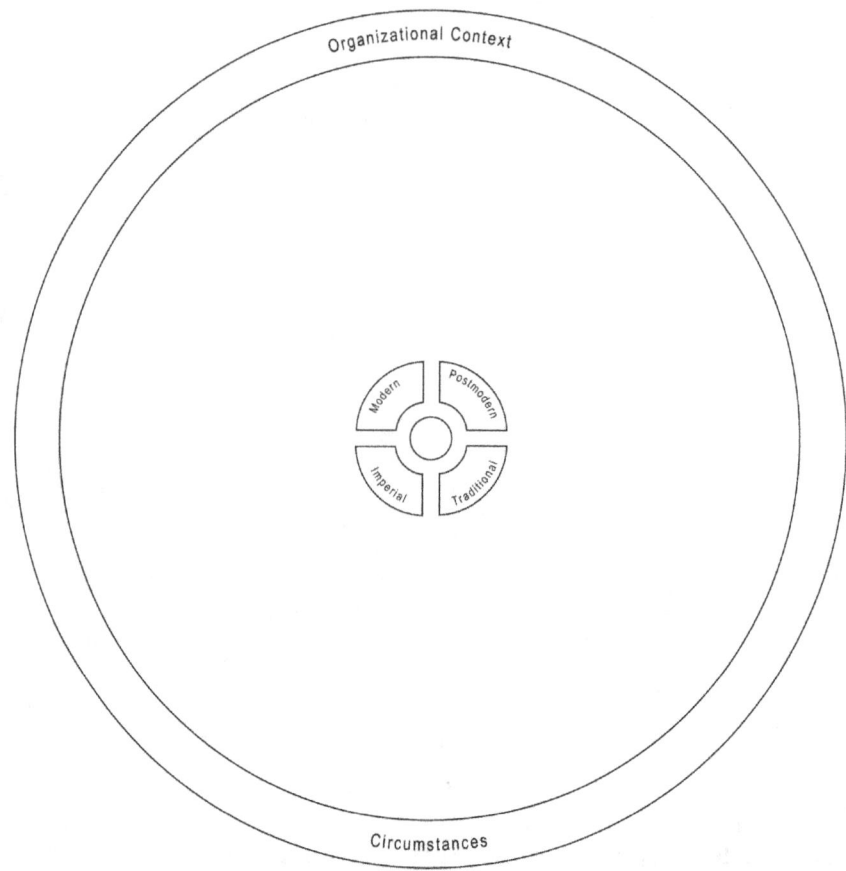

The follower worldviews will let us know which style(s) of leadership we should be emphasizing. We illustrate this with the four leadership styles, always paired correctly with the follower worldviews.

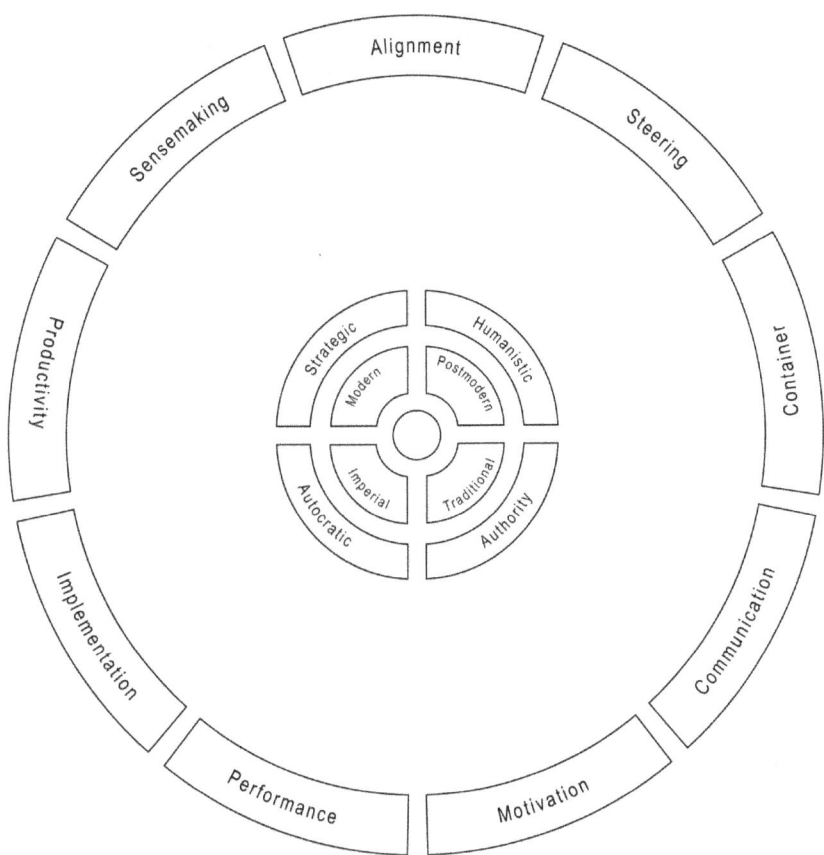

At this point, you know what comes next. Leaders have inherent leadership responsibilities, and "essential abilities" they draw upon to fulfill those responsibilities. The way they approach those responsibilities (and how those abilities are expressed) are a function of their "leadership style."

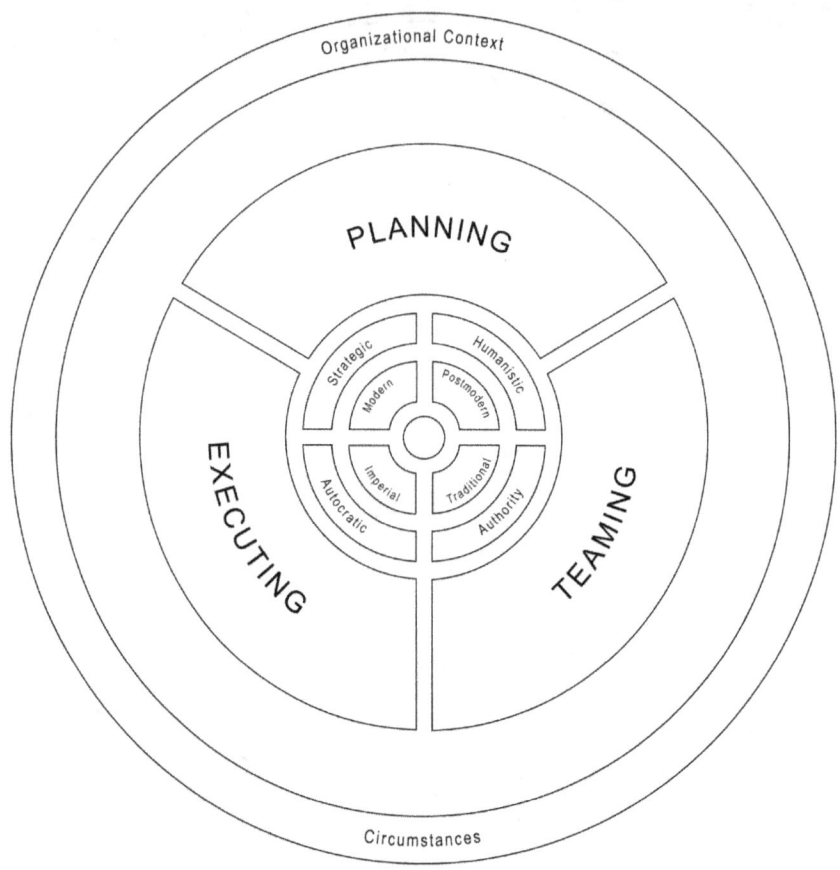

Finally, we know that leaders must engage many activities, and use their "skill sets" in order to fulfill those responsibilities. Of course each of these skill sets looks different according to the leadership style being used. Once we bring the nine skill sets back in, we have the full Universal Leadership Model.

In the next chapter, we will take a much closer look at how leaders engage these three abilities and nine core practices using one of four different leadership styles that must be paired with the worldview of the follower to be effective. After that, we will take a more granular look at the nine skill sets and the practices and techniques we deploy under each.

CHAPTER 6:
USING THE RIGHT STYLE WITH THE RIGHT FOLLOWERS

A person's worldview dictates how they see the world, what they believe is true about the world and the people in it, and what they value.

For leaders to be viewed as credible, they must match the correct leadership style with the followers' worldview. This is the key to all "resonant" leadership.

When a leader uses a leadership style that is associated with a worldview different from the follower's, this signals to the follower that this leader "doesn't get it."

Put another way, the follower sees the leader as out of touch, clueless, not understanding what is really important, or not getting how the world really works.

A lack of "worldview alignment" results in the follower seeing the leader as not credible, not competent, or in the worst case, not trustworthy.

This is the key to what Ken Wilber and our academic colleagues call "integral leadership" which is another word for integrally-informed leadership, that is, leadership that is informed by integral psychology.

This is one of the main things that sets the Accelerating Leadership approach to leadership development apart from most of the other leadership learning methods available in the market. Our approach to leadership is informed by a nuanced understanding of psychology, in particular, integral psychology which incorporates developmental psychology, worldviews and value systems, all of which are essential for effective leadership.

This chapter is about accurately recognizing worldviews and matching them with the respective universal leadership style. Think of this "matching" activity as an actual (relatively advanced) leadership practice.

After teaching this practice to thousands of executives in corporate America, I can tell you with experience and authority that this leadership practice has the power to unlock and amplify the potency of the other principles and practices associated with leadership.

Using the right "leadership style" that matches the follower's (or team's) worldview amplifies the effectiveness of every other technique described in this book and the other three books in this series.

Leadership sensemaking is most fundamentally about "perspective taking."

An integral approach to leadership involves using numerous frameworks as "lenses" which provide visibility into dimensions of reality that conventional leaders are unaware of, overlook, or ignore. The result of these superior (more accurate) lenses and precision perspective-taking practices is greater awareness, better approaches, and more skillful action.

While "matching styles with mindsets" is central to Accelerating Leadership, it does not represent the totality of it. Rather, it provides a logical and helpful orienting framework—like the conventions of North, South, East, West on a geographical map—to ensure that the leader is headed in the right direction.

As you read this chapter, please be mindful of the fact that this is merely an introduction, a high-level overview of this framework. The goal is for you to become familiar with it. The application of these leadership styles (to all of the different abilities and skill sets) will come with time. It should be obvious that understanding the mindset of your followers (or your team or culture) is central to leadership effectiveness. In fact, most comprehensive leader development programs teach some methods for "understanding people."

Some simply teach listening skills, many teach various kinds of personality typology systems, and a few use stages of development (a.k.a. stages of psychological maturity) to help leaders better understand their followers and what makes them tick.

I'm going to use an American idiom—being "in the ballpark"—as an analogy to illustrate a crucial point.

Those personality types, situational leadership tactics, and get-to-know-your-people methods are like finding your section and seat at a large baseball game.

Assuming that you are in the correct stadium, knowing the exact section, row and seat number is very helpful. But here's the catch. In this analogy, your followers' worldview (their values and universal beliefs) represents the stadium. If you fail to accurately recognize your followers' worldview, then you are not even in the right ballpark; therefore, the details about personality types and behavioral tendencies (even a person's goals) are essentially useless.

Worldview is the overall perspective from which one sees and interprets the world.

> *A person's worldview defines what they care about, what motivates them, what they believe is worthwhile, and what they believe lacks value or is "wrong." And as we now understand it also specifically dictates which leadership style they will resonant with, and follow, as well as which approaches are likely to backfire.*

If you want to understand people, you first need to get "into the right ballpark" by identifying their worldview.

I believe that the failure to grasp meaning making systems—what I am calling worldviews here—lies at the heart of the problem with conventional approaches to leadership. Those approaches often wrongly assume that people's motivations are homogenous. Most conventional approaches to leadership (and also management) fail to adequately take into account the fact that people with different worldviews value different things, interpret the same facts differently, and subsequently have very different priorities. This mistake is at the heart of the "bogus leadership advice" most so-called experts offer.

Follower Mindsets Are the Key to Leadership Success

I mentioned Barbara Kellerman (Bad Leadership, The End of Leadership and Professionalizing Leadership) and Jeffrey Pfeffer (Leadership BS) in the introduction. Unfortunately, these two courageous "whistleblowers" are among only a few leadership experts that are acknowledging the fact that most leadership development programs focus mainly on the leader and generally avoid largely or completely the "context" in which the leadership is occurring. Worse, they almost all leave the followers out of the equation altogether.

Yes, you read that right. The vast majority of leadership training programs mostly or completely ignore the followers! They focus the vast majority of the time talking about traits of great leaders and qualities of effective leaders with seemingly no awareness at all of the needs, worldviews and preferences of the followers. This, again, is one of the main reasons that most leadership development programs produce such criminally dismal results. In her books, Kellerman really takes the leadership industry to talk over this colossal error. She underscores the fact that any legitimate approach to leadership must take into account all three elements of the leader, the context (the circumstances), and especially the followers.

I would suggest that the most important part of the context, the circumstances, is the follower's worldview. If you understand the follower's worldview (or mindset as I call it), then you will know what they care about, what is important to them, how they define leadership, and what they look for in a person they view as a credible leader.

Most importantly, if you know a person's "follower mindset," and you know how to match up the mindsets with the four Universal Leadership Styles, then you can avoid the embarrassing situation of using the wrong style with the wrong person and destroying your leadership credibility in their eyes.

As I have stated before, in the same way that beauty is in the eye of the beholder, leadership is in the eye of the follower. If you use the wrong leadership style with the wrong person, they will not see you as a credible leader. They will see you as clueless or even foolish.

A leadership approach that is extremely resonant with one employee, team or department will be ineffective or even offensive for another.

The troublesome issue is: "How can you know which approach will be effective and which will be offensive?"
The answer, of course, is the follower's worldview.

As I mentioned in the section where I introduced the Leadership Rosetta Stone, integral psychology shows us that about 95% of the values/belief systems that today's leaders are likely to encounter fall into four broad worldviews.

For some readers, this fact is not new. Many readers are already familiar with *Modern, Postmodern,* and *Traditional* worldviews. However, few people are aware of the fact that these "value systems" predict with astonishing accuracy which leadership style will be resonant and appreciated, and which styles will be met with resistance and/or rejection.

It is hard to overstate the significance of this. This realization lies at the heart of the breakthrough that my team discovered, with Ken Wilber's guidance in the early 2000s. Essentially, this deceptively simple Universal Leadership Model successfully aggregates, synthesizes, and integrates, more than a 100 years of leadership theories. Moreover, once sufficiently internalized in practice (and that takes a little time of course), this unique leadership framework allows leaders to effectively motivate and influence followers (of all kinds) with a level of precision and efficacy that is rarely witnessed.

Also, this works everywhere it has been tested. In corporate environments, financial services, construction sites, assembly lines, hospitals, police forces, military... even in remote African tribal villages.

Values Research

Worldviews are composed of values and universal beliefs. Values are perceptual filters minds use to determine ("evaluate") what is important in any given situation. Universal beliefs are broad-based beliefs about self, others, and system (how the world is perceived to work). In terms of knowing which leader a given person is likely to follow (or elect given the choice), in terms of knowing what people care about, in terms of knowing what motivates people, in terms of understanding people in the most fundamental sense, nothing is more germane than values.

The conceptualization and use of values models is widespread and informed by a multitude of different approaches that differ in details but are quite similar in principle and overarching conclusions. Values research is widely used by psychologists, political scientists, and marketers. The pervasive role of values in all aspects of human life has motivated hundreds of studies in the disciplines of psychology, sociology, cultural anthropology, and consumer behavior.

A large body of research has shown conclusively that values represent both a powerful explanation of and influence on a variety of individual and collective behaviors. In fact, in recent years, the study and measurement of values has become one of the most dynamic research areas in the social science disciplines (management, leadership, marketing and consumer behavior). Several values measurement methodologies are currently available and more are surfacing.

These worldviews, along with their correlating universal leadership styles, cut across nationalities, ethnicity, and culture.

There is nothing inherently American or North American (or European or Caucasian) about these worldviews and leadership styles. However, I live in the U.S. and most of my work has involved leaders in the Americas. The examples and illustrations in my teaching reflect my experience. Also, in this presentation,

I often use the term "mindset" in place of or in addition to the more academic term "worldview."

When describing people who hold a worldview, it is often helpful to use the word "mindset" in place of the word worldview. Rather than say, this person holds a modern worldview, we could say, this person has a "modern mindset" or better still, this person has an "achiever mindset." This section of the book will follow this convention and will use "mindset" in place of "worldview."

This presentation uses broad and simplified examples of single worldviews or mindsets that help new students become familiar with their basic appearance and function. Once you can begin to recognize them, in time you will begin to see how they can be combined (as some people's mindset is a blend of two such as 50/50 or 60/40).

Next, I will go through each of the four follower mindsets, describe how the world looks through that lens, refer to the massive amount of research that backs up these assertions, and give you several examples of "profiles" of employees who typify this mindset. After the explanation of the follower mindset, then I will offer a more detailed explanation of the style of leadership that should be used with people with that mindset.

Modern Worldview

People with a modern worldview can also be described as having an "Achiever mindset." They identify with being highly rational, competitive, ambitious, autonomous and elite. They emphasize success and/or status as defined by material acquisition and "upward mobility."

They value excellence, advancement, prosperity, achievement, and status. Most importantly, they prefer to follow leaders who are perceived to have the most expertise and ability to achieve goals. In other words, they follow leaders who use the Strategic Leadership style.

The Achiever mindset (and the Strategic Leadership style) is well suited for the following environments and circumstances: sales departments, professional services firms, innovation-driven organizations, senior management positions, and in roles that require advanced levels of education such as scientific research.

Seeing the World Through a Modern Lens

In academic circles, this worldview is referred to as the "Modern worldview" (as contrasted to the Traditional and Postmodern worldviews).

When you look at the world through this lens, you see a playing field full of possibilities to explore and opportunities to achieve. You will emphasize the scientific and rational dimensions of what you see. The key to life is to strive for, and achieve "success."

Through this lens, it becomes easy to believe in the advancement of humankind through the application of the highly disciplined rational mind and its scientific, technological, and medical manifestations. Life is to be met and mastered by finding the best way to act on its limitless opportunities.

Empirical Research

While this worldview, or "follower mindset" may be new for a few readers, there is nothing new, novel or controversial about it; in fact, my descriptions are based on widely-accepted and respected empirical research that has come out of Harvard, Yale, Boston College, Washington University and other top institutions over the last four decades. I offer more nuanced, academic analysis in other books (especially my book series on Integral Leadership). For our purposes here, I will merely highlight the academic terms that the different leading psychologists use for this worldview (follower mindset). McClelland uses the term "Achievement," Loevinger uses "Conscientious," Kohlberg uses "Social Order," Graves uses "Multiplistic-Achievist," Kegan uses "Institutional," Wade uses "Achievement," and Torbert uses "Achiever." When I'm using "follower mindset" terminology, I say "Achiever" mindset and when I'm using the worldview term, I call it the "Modern" worldview. Although I don't use Ken Wilber's color schemes in this book created for mainstream readers, for my readers who are students of integral theory, I will mention here that the Wilberian color code for this worldview is "orange."

Understanding People with a Modern Worldview

People with this mindset tend to believe that while there are many valid ways to think and behave, there is always one best way. People with this mindset want to feel they are at the "top of their game" and that they have earned (quite literally, in some cases) the recognition of belonging to an elite group.

They are not satisfied to simply "play by the rules;" rather, they want to fully understand the rules to gain a competitive advantage over those with less acuity, with the ultimate ambition of becoming so successful that they might eventually "change the rules of the game." Many of their decisions will be motivated by the promise of success and status, as well as an awareness and fairly sophisticated understanding of the dynamics of the overall system within which they operate (company, church, nation, global marketplace).

Some examples of occupational roles that tend to epitomize the Achiever mindset include salespeople, attorneys, research scientists, marketing agents, PR and advertising representatives, elected public officials, architects, and physicians in conventional practice (as opposed to alternative medicine which would very likely be someone with a Pluralistic mindset described in the next section). Following are some example profiles of people with these mindsets.

Rob - Research Scientist

I'm a research scientist who's convinced that most of the world's problems can be solved with the right technological advancements and tools. I think that many people hold superstitious, irrational beliefs that are detrimental to society's interests and retard scientific progress. While I enjoy my work during the week, I pursue my real passion on the weekends. I've completed over twenty triathlons and placed in the top five in most of them. My training schedule could probably qualify as some sort of third world form of punishment, but when I cross the finish line in first place it's all worth it. There's a force in me that's relentless in its determination to win. There's something exhilarating about testing your limits and pushing your personal edge.

Danielle - Attorney

I just graduated from Harvard Law School and I am joining one of the most prestigious firms in the country. I grew up in a two-parent working class household and was a latch-key kid. My parents were focused on providing necessities for us. They helped me to see that hard work and determination are keys to success. While I respect my parent's "traditional" ways, I knew from a young age that I wanted to work smarter, not harder, to enjoy the finer things in life. And while my parents' religious orientation works for them, I wasn't satisfied with simplistic answers to complex questions. To be honest, I believe that the world would be a better place if more people would put their faith in reason and look to science rather than religion for answers.

Lee - Small Business Owner

I own a small web-based company that produces and sells custom laptop cases for the fashion-conscious consumer. As a start-up, I wasn't entirely sure what I was doing but decided to take some calculated risks while telling myself that failing wasn't an option. I became incredibly focused and goal-oriented, and within two years I was featured as Entrepreneur of the Year in a nation-wide magazine.

Strategic Leadership

People like Lee, Danielle and Rob who have a modern worldview prefer to follow leaders who embody personal excellence and success and who are perceived to be most likely to achieve predefined goals.

In this form of leadership, the person with the most expertise leads via strategic planning and aligned incentives. It is characterized by incentivizing teams to execute well-conceived plans to outperform their competitors. In academic terms, this approach is sometimes referred to as "transactional" to differentiate it from the "transformational" quality of the Collaborative Leadership style.

It's easy to see how followers with this "Achiever mindset" finds this strategic, goal-oriented leadership approach resonant. In fact, as we shall see, the developers and advocates of the many "schools of leadership" that fall into this category nearly always possess the corresponding worldview.

This explains why academics / researchers / authors who are enthusiastic proponents of each leadership style believe that their style is the best and should be used in every situation.

When you are with a group of people who share the same values system, if you pay attention to their language you will notice that they have a way of communicating with each other that reflects their common values and beliefs.

My mentor Ken Wilber refers to this as the "Dominant Mode of Discourse." I use the shorter term "Values Dialect" (or simply dialect). This values dialect is the dialect of business.

Leaders whose primary worldview is Postmodern or Traditional and who want to be taken seriously in business need to learn to speak this "modern worldview" (or "Achiever") dialect even if it is not their "native tongue."

Postmodern Worldview

People with a postmodern worldview, also called an "Affiliative" mindset identify with being nonjudgmental, egalitarian, and socially and environmentally conscious.

They value connection, tolerance, cultural sensitivity, diversity, sustainability, and interdependence. They strive for fulfillment as defined by personal growth, increased awareness, harmonious relationships, and "making a difference."

Most importantly, they prefer to follow leaders who are perceived as being aware, sensitive to the wellbeing of others, value consensus, and always treat others as equals; in other words, leaders who use a Humanistic leadership style. My colleagues and I also refer to this style as the "Collaborative" leadership style. I will use both terms in this book series.

Seeing the World Through a Postmodern Lens

In academic circles, this worldview is referred to as the "Postmodern Worldview" (as contrasted with the Modern or Traditional). It is sometimes also called a "pluralistic" worldview.

Sociologist and bestselling author Paul Ray uses the term "Cultural Creatives" to describe people who identify with the worldview. In his book *The Cultural Creatives: How 50 Million People Are Changing the World*, he summarizes research on 50 million adult Americans (slightly over one quarter of the adult population). Ray presents a significant amount of demographic and psychographic research comparing and contrasting this worldview to the Traditional worldview and Modern worldview. *Developmental Politics: How America Can Grow Into a Better Version of Itself,* written by my colleague from Integral Institute, Steve Mcintosh, is another excellent book that compares and contrasts these same worldviews.

When you look at the world through this Postmodern lens, you see a diverse ecosystem where cooperation leads to synergy. The Postmodern worldview is often described as "pluralistic." The dictionary definition of pluralistic is: "a social perspective that believes no single explanatory system or view of reality can account for all the phenomena of life; rather there are many (plural) truths.

Further, it is desirable to have numerous distinct ethnic, religious, or cultural groups present and tolerated in society."

You know many people with this Postmodern (or pluralistic) worldview. You can easily identify by their strongly held values of diversity, equality and inclusion, and their strong dislike of hierarchy and patriarchy. Right-wing (conservative) critics refer derogatorily to this worldview (and the subculture that it has spawned) as "woke."

Empirical Research

My descriptions in this book are all based on empirical research out of Harvard, Yale, Boston College, Washington University and other top institutions over the last four decades. For this short book, I will simply mention the academic terms that the different leading psychologists use for this worldview / follower mindset. McClelland uses the term "Affiliative," Wade also uses "Affiliative," Loevinger uses "Individualistic," Kohlberg uses "Social Contract," Graves uses "Relativistic-Personalistic," Kegan uses "late-institutional" into "early-Interindividual," and Torbert uses "Individualist." When I'm using the "follower mindset" convention, I say "Affiliative" mindset. and when using the worldview term, I say "Postmodern" worldview. Although I don't use Ken Wilber's color schemes in this book created for mainstream readers, for my readers who are students of integral theory, I will mention here that the Wilberian color code for this worldview is "green."

Understanding People with a Postmodern Worldview

Historically, leaders with the postmodern worldview were responsible for the human rights and environmental movements.

This includes the Women's Rights movement, the Equality Movement, and the LGBTQ Movement. We saw this worldview (and mindset) first explode onto the scene in the 1960s. We have seen this "progressive" worldview gain popularity again in the 2000s. It is the predominant worldview in most liberal arts colleges, Ivy League institutions of higher education, and much of academia.

People with this "Affiliative" mindset tend to display egalitarian, tolerant attitudes, and are often enthusiastic endorsers of equal rights and equal opportunity for all people in all situations. As I mentioned before, you can easily recognize them as they champion what they refer to as diversity, equity and inclusion (or DEI for short). You can also recognize them by their enthusiastic criticism of hierarchy and patriarchy.

People with this mindset are far more motivated about "making a difference" than "making money" and this is very puzzling to "Achievers" (who often wrongly assume everyone is primarily motivated by money).

Whereas, people with the Achiever mindset emphasize external/material accomplishments (financial success, material acquisitions, status), people with this Affiliative mindset prefer to emphasize internal/intangible accomplishments (awareness, human connection, emotional fulfillment). As such, they are more motivated by personal growth, people, and relationships than by material gain.

Of course, this group can be highly motivated to achieve material success for a social or environmental cause as long as this is accomplished without sacrifices of personal growth or rewarding relationships. People with this Affiliative mindset tend to make decisions motivated by the belief that their choice will help them (or their organization) continue to grow and develop, and that the world will be positively impacted (or at least not negatively affected) by their actions. They want to avoid harming others, including animals, and are often motivated by "reducing their carbon footprint." People with this mindset gravitate toward communities that value tolerance for multiple perspectives, interdependence, creativity, diversity, activism, and "progressive" approaches of all kinds. They prefer nontraditional, "humanized" workplaces where self-expression is encouraged and rewarded; where contribution to social, political, and environmental causes is mission-critical or intrinsic to profitability; where duties and roles are actively interchanged in the service of a nonhierarchical, egalitarian approach; where team and roundtable gatherings are standard to internal operations and decision-making; where the job requires higher education; and where ongoing growth and development along with "work-life-balance" are encouraged.

A book that is aimed squarely at Affiliative readers and that does a great job of describing these "humanized" workplaces while strongly advocating for the non-hierarchical "self-managed teams" approach and the Humanistic leadership style is entitled, *"Reinventing Organizations: A Guide to Creating Organizations Inspired by the Next Stage in Human Consciousness."* If you want to read about companies that have adopted the Humanistic leadership style and the "self-managed teams" approach, read this book. But I must caution you if you plan to read *Reinventing Organizations.*

> *The author of Reinventing Organizations, Frederic Laloux confuses readers by referring to the self-managed teams, humanized workplace approach as the "Teal Organization." The reason that this is confusing is because it is flatly wrong. Wilber introduced the color "Teal" as a convention for "Integral" approaches. Self-managed teams are not "Integral" and definitely not "Teal." They only work for Postmodern workforces and are disastrous with workforces with predominantly Traditional or Imperial worldviews*

I go into much more detail in my book: *Integral Leadership: The World's First Unifying Theory of Leadership That Will Forever Transform How You Understand, Practice and Develop Leadership*. I feel compelled to mention it here in case you read Laloux's book which is an excellent example of Humanistic leadership (for Postmodern workers). Just understand that a "Teal" or "Integral" approach to leadership and organizations is precisely what I describe in my numerous books about Integral Leadership.

I will highlight the center of the model here as a refresher.

An integral approach to leadership and organizational design always pairs the correct leadership style (and organizational structure) with the mindset (values, beliefs, needs and preferences) of the followers who the leader wishes to influence (or support or serve).

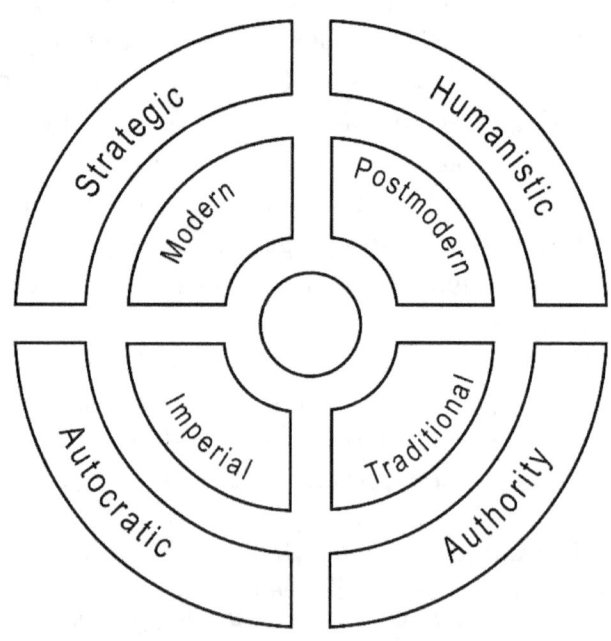

Frederick Laloux and many other writers, who are burdened by strong unconscious Postmodern worldview biases, make the mistake of trying to push a Humanistic (self-managed teams) approach on followers who do not have a Postmodern worldview. This is not only ill-advised, wrong-headed and very costly, its actually cruel.

> *A Humanistic, self-managed teams approach literally causes Traditional workers to underperform and often fail. This is the polar `opposite of "setting people up to succeed." This is the definition of setting people up to fail.*

Dispite what Laloux recommends in his book Reinventing Organizations, there is nothing "Teal" or "Integral" about trying to force a "self-managed teams approach" (which only ever works with workers with an Postmodern worldview) onto workers who have an *Imperial, Traditional or Modern* worldview. Many have tried and every single one of them has failed. It NEVER works to use the postmodern "self-managed team" (a.k.a. "Inclusive" leadership style) with people with Imperial, Traditional or Modern worldviews.

There is another popular and somewhat controversial theory and approach to organizational structures called "holacracy" that replaces hierarchy with concentric circles, self-managed teams, and shared decision making.

It works adequately well with companies that are made up exclusively of workers with the Postmodern worldview (a.k.a. Affiliative mindset), but when this structure is attempted with organizations that are comprised of a significant population of the other three mindsets, it usually fails. Its most famous failure was with the well-known shoe company, Zappos.

This is another example of the common mistake that Laloux (and many others) make. I will state it again. People with unconscious Postmodern worldview bias often try to push the "Humanistic" leadership style and the "self-managed teams" organizational approach onto workforces that are not strictly (or even primarily) Postmodern (or Affiliative). This mistake results in failure 100% of the time.

Even more puzzling is the fact that many proponents of this "Humanistic" leadership style and this "self-managed teams" organizational structure wrongly think that they are "Integral" or that they have an "Integral" worldview merely because they read books by Integral theorists such as my mentor Ken Wilber and many of my colleagues. This is one of the reasons that the "Integral Movement" as it is called has stumbled and often produced disappointing results.

Many people who identify as "Integral" are actually students of Integral theory and may have meta-systemic (or Teal) "cognition," but are definitely Postmodern in their values and worldview. This creates a whole host of problems, including what I call "bogus leadership advice."

> *Trust me on this. My 22+ years working in organizations shows that an "Integral" approach to leadership and to organizational design is always defined as matching the right leadership style or organizational structure to the worldviews/mindsets of the workforce. Any time someone is strongly advocating a Humanistic or "self-managed teams" approach for a workforce that is not Postmodern / Affiliative, then that advocate is pushing their own unconscious worldview bias onto those people who don't share that worldview. That is literally the opposite of an "Integral" (or "Teal") approach.*

An Integral (or "Teal") approach to leadership is defined by "meeting people where they are and supporting them accordingly." An Integral approach would never, ever impose an unconscious Postmodern worldview bias onto people who don't share that worldview as Frederick Laloux does in his otherwise excellent book about self-managed teams, *Reinventing Organizations*.

Pardon the short "rant," but this is really important and I don't want you to make a fool of yourself by pushing Humanistic leadership and self-managed teams approaches onto people and organizations that will result in you destroying your credibility, damaging team morale, and potentially costing your company millions of dollars in losses. While "inclusive leadership" is currently popular with many people, especially Postmodern coaches, trainers and consultants, it should be used sparingly and primarily or exclusively with followers (and teams) with a Postmodern worldview.

Now that I have finished telling my "cautionary tale," let's continue our conversation about really understanding people with a Postmodern worldview and an Affiliative mindset.

If the people you serve, or a subset of them, display this Postmodern worldview (and values) and have this Affiliative mindset (as the profiles that follow clearly do), then they will respond very positively to the Humanistic leadership style (that I will describe in more nuanced detail in a moment).

To help cement your understanding, I want to introduce you to three typical worker profiles of people who have a strong, predominant Affiliative mindset. I am certain one of these profiles (if not more than one) will remind you of someone you know!

Pay attention to the patterns I'm describing, they are all around you, and the sooner you begin to recognize them, the sooner you will know which leadership style or approach will be resonant with them!

Jonathan - Volunteer

Right out of college I joined the Peace Corps. At some point during my senior year, I realized that most of the world's population will never have the opportunities I once took for granted. Today, I work as a diversity consultant in the public sector, I help people within organizations accept and find strength in each other's differences. There's a real tendency in all of us to feel that our own way of looking at things is intrinsically superior, and it's this attitude that is responsible for most of the world's conflict. If everyone would accept each other's differences, we'd finally have a peaceful planet.

Delia - Record Label Owner

At eighteen, I founded my own music label because I wanted to promote social justice and retain artistic integrity that a corporate mentality wouldn't allow. After selling over 50,000 of my albums, the major labels came courting with huge deals. Because they wanted me to compromise, I declined. Today, my label is an internationally known icon for independent art, political action, and grassroots sponsorship.

Larry - Physician

I'm an MD and the founder of a holistic health care company that's committed to people and the planet first and profit second. I've taken great care to give everyone in my organization an equal voice; there is no hierarchy to speak of, and decision-making is done by consensus. As far as I'm concerned, a good business should function a lot like a democracy to ensure that too much power isn't invested in any one person. It's clear to me that the modern lifestyle being commercialized and unrelentingly promoted by megacorporations is environmentally unsustainable for the planet. When I recognized I was part of the problem, I decided to become part of the solution by simplifying my life and limiting my consumption.

Humanistic Leadership

People like Larry, Delia and Jonathan who have an Affiliative mindset prefer to follow leaders who are perceived as being aware, sensitive to the wellbeing of others, value consensus, and always treat others, even the lowest paid employee, as equals.

Followers who have this Affiliative mindset believe that leadership is not vested in any single person; rather, it should be consensus-based in the sense that self-managed teams should lead themselves.

I'm hoping that at this point in this conversation the light bulb is coming on. This should be starting to make perfect sense. It is logical, reasonable, and also true and accurate.

As I have pointed out previously, this "Humanistic" leadership approach is considered "transformational" and involves inviting people's perceptions, feelings and intuition via roundtable discussion and dialog to arrive at consensus, then work collaboratively toward common goals that serve the greater good. This style of leadership is also called "Transformational leadership" and "Collaborative" leadership.

For people like Larry, Delia and Jonathan, and the many people you have in your life with similar mindsets, leadership is not based on positional authority (or a title), but rather, it is understood to be situational and temporary. For Affiliative mindset followers, nearly all position-based authority is viewed as highly questionable or even rejected outright. Remember, people with a predominant Affiliative mindset elevate diversity, equity and inclusion to the highest level of values and they tend to despise hierarchy because they wrongly assume all forms of hierarchy are "dominator hierarchies" created by the patriarchy and reflect "systemic racism." Of course there is a kernel of truth in most things, and dominator hierarchies, and certainly racism and patriarchal approaches are as outdated as the Bronze Age belief systems they stem from.

However, it should be obvious to most reasonable people that hierarchies are built into nature, they are natural and are a natural way for organizations to be structured.

Clearly it is best that more experienced, more seasoned, more knowledgeable, higher trained and more competent people should have more authority to make decisions on behalf of the organization. In a family unit you don't give children the same authority and decision making power as the adults.

Hierarchies are natural and not all hierarchies are "dominator hierarchies," patriarchal or reflections of "systemic racism." When people push these extreme, inaccurate and divisive views, they are merely projecting their unconscious worldview bias.

Recall that workers with a Traditional mindset not only prefer hierarchy, a strict code of right and wrong, clear consequences and firm punishment of rule breakers, they actually require hierarchy and its associated strict "chain of command" to function well. When the modern organizational structure called the "matrix organization" is installed with Traditional workers, requiring them to have not one but two bosses, it quickly unravels. Traditional workers need one boss, a clear hierarchy to be happy and productive. Self-managed teams are an unmitigated disaster when imposed on Traditional workers.

I am taking the time in this conversation to draw this contrast between an "Authority" approach and a "Humanistic" to help you have a more clear grasp of the needs and preferences of workers like Larry, Delia and Jonathan who have this Affiliative mindset. Their leadership needs and preferences could not be more different than the profiles of John, Susan and Daniel that you will mee in the next section and who reflect the Traditional mindset.

Returning to the Humanistic leadership style so popular with Affiliative workers (and readers), many of the books that promote work-life balance, emotionally-aware "resonant" leadership, and "appreciative inquiry" are both popular with people with this Affiliative mindset and were written by people with Affiliative mindsets.

Katzenbach and Smith's bestselling book, *The Wisdom of Teams*, was mentioned earlier in this book

When authors are subject to their own worldview (and fail to recognize the different worldviews at play in the workplace), they tend to advocate their approach as the best approach. Katzenbach and Smith believe that "only self-managed teams are real teams" and even say in their books that "single-leader led teams are not real teams." I think they make my point for me with these statements that reflect a deep unconscious Postmodern worldview bias.

Humanistic leadership, also called collaborative leadership and transformational leadership, is currently in the vanguard of popular business literature. For many leaders, this humanistic, transformational approach is a welcome shift away from the transactional and traditional (authority) approaches that have been popular for so long. However, integrally informed leaders see the flaw in this thinking. There is no best leadership approach for all types of people. This line of thinking leaves the followers out of the leadership equation or it assumes all followers have a single homogeneous mindset and eliminates the possibility of a diverse group of followers. Again, this is unconscious worldview bias at its worst. I will remind you once more...

The best leadership approach is always the one that will be most resonant with the people you hope to lead.

Humanistic leadership works great with people with Affiliative mindsets. However, people with an Achiever mindset consider it to be too touchy-feely, people with a Traditional mindset consider "relativistic values" to be immoral, and people with a Power mindset interpret kindness and sensitivity as weaknesses and will steamroll right over it. This is one of the reasons Holacracy failed.

Whenever there were workers in the organization with an Imperial or Modern worldview (Power or Achiever mindsets), they would manipulate the self-managed teams decision-making structure for their own "power" or "competitive advantage" (respectively based on the mindset). Holacracy works fairly well when the organization is made up of predominantly Postmodern (Affiliative) workers, and can work with Modern (Achiever) workers, but quickly unravels in organizations with Traditional or Imperial workforces.

Now let's shift this conversation to the workers with a that Traditional mindset I have contrasting with the Affiliative mindset.

The Traditional Mindset

People with a Traditional Mindset identify with being responsible, purposeful, self-sufficient and self-sacrificing. They seek a reassuring sense of stability, security, and belonging by conforming to a worldview that they unambiguously describe as the tried and true "natural order of things."

This so-called "natural order of things" is always defined by the long-standing traditions of the culture in which they were socialized. So the natural order is defined by the Bible for Traditional Christians, the Torah for Orthodox Jews and the Koran for Traditional Muslims. For people with this Traditional worldview who live in China, the "natural order of things" is defined by the Communist Party of China. For people with a Traditional worldview, the "natural order of things" and as Integral pioneer Clare Graves called it, the "one right way to think and behave" is always defined by the "higher authority" which may be the Communist Party, the Bible, the Torah or the Koran depending on their parents beliefs and/or the traditions and culture in which they were socialized (and have not deviated from even as educated adults).

As logic and reason would lead you to expect, people with this Traditional mindset always strongly prefer to follow leaders who are perceived as having positional and/or moral authority; in other words, leaders who use an Authority leadership style (which also goes by the label Bureaucratic leadership style).

Seeing the World Through a Traditional Lens

As I have mentioned and should be abundantly obvious, the "Traditional worldview" is contrasting it with the so-called "Modern" and "Postmodern"

worldviews across countless books, papers and academic writings. These terms are widely accepted by sociologists, psychologists and frankly nearly all social scientists.

When you look through the "Traditional lens," as I will call it, you see an ordered existence under the control of a higher authority and ultimate Truth.

Although amber is the integral theory color code we associate with this worldview, when you look through the Traditional lens, what you actually see is a black-and-white, concrete, literal, fundamentalist, dualistic world of right and wrong, insiders and outsiders, believers and non-believers, and good and evil.

Workers with this Traditional worldview believe that people who conform to rigid traditional roles (such as the man earning money and the woman staying home and raising children) as following the "natural order of things." Further, they believe that people who exercise their freedom of choice to deviate from these conventional roles, such as people who are "gender fluid," non-binary, or transexual or even "progressive" or "liberal" as an aberration at best and evil at worst.

If you know what to look for it is very easy to spot people with this Traditional mindset. Magazines, books, television and social media is riddled with these Traditional views. There are entire television and radio networks set up to make billions of dollars off the market that Traditional viewers make up. Of course, for most readers I'm pointing out something that is fairly obvious. But this is not often written about or talked about, and it is very rare for any actual leadership experts to even mention this! So I'm taking the time here in our "conversation" to point out these really essential distinctions.

Empirical Research

My descriptions in this book are all based on empirical research from Harvard, Yale, Boston College, Washington University and other top institutions over the last four decades. For our purposes here, I will merely mention the academic terms that the different leading psychologists use for this worldview and follower mindset. McClelland uses the term "Authority," Loevinger uses "Conformist," Kohlberg uses "Interpersonal Accord" and "Conformity," Graves uses "Absolutistic-Obedience," Kegan uses "Interpersonal," Wade uses "Conformist," and Torbert uses "Diplomat." I use the familiar word Traditional for both the worldview and the follower mindset. Although I don't use Ken Wilber's color schemes in this book written for a mainstream audience for my readers who are students of Integral theory, I will mention here that the Wilberian color code for this worldview is "amber." Also some readers may be familiar with the National Values Center (Spiral Dynamics) colors, which is "blue" for this mindset.

Understanding People with a Traditional Mindset

People with Traditional mindsets tend to be dedicated, reliable, loyal, responsible, conscientious, and can be expected to think and act in routine, predictable ways. They are oriented around learning and following the rules defined by authority, and are more than willing to subjugate their own impulses and desires in the service of a greater calling, cause, or mission that they find meaningful, purposeful and in accord with their traditional beliefs.

While "Blue Collar jobs" are typical, people with this mindset are especially attracted to work that promotes what they consider to be the moral good (e.g., ministers, teachers, police officers, guidance counselors, children's athletic coaches, etc.). In addition to preferring jobs that require routine and discipline, this group thrives in circumstances that others might view as repetitive or tedious. Consequently, workers with this mindset usually excel in "standards" and "compliance" and "quality control" roles as well as organizational and system maintenance jobs.

Unlike people with the Affiliative mindset, workers with this Traditional mindset value hierarchy, expect hierarchy, need hierarchy and thrive in a hierarchical system. As mentioned in the section about Humanistic leadership, unless you want to destroy your credibility, damage morale and potentially cost your company millions of dollars in losses, never ever ever attempt to eliminate hierarchy and impose "self-managed teams" on a workforce made up predominantly of people with a Traditional worldview.

People with a Traditional mindset respond best (and perform best) with clearly defined rules, deadlines, responsibilities and a well-defined chain of command.

Traditional workers appreciate a written code of conduct to refer to, especially one that offers clear protocols for action and predictable consequences for success and failure. Wherever in the world you encounter this Traditional worldview, it will define acceptable and unacceptable gender roles, sexual orientations and practices, food and drink consumption, and of course spiritual practices based on the long-standing traditions endemic to the culture they were raised in.

As Integral pioneer Clare Graves explained, people with this Traditional mindset believe tht "there is one and only one right way to think and behave."

To the Traditional worker, conforming to authority's prescribed "right" way to think and behave is the key to ensure future rewards.

> *It is very important to understand that while the nitty-gritty details of the local customs, culture and religious practices will naturally differ, the broad-based core values and the universal beliefs (about self, others and system) that comprise the Traditional worldview will be identical anywhere on the planet, whether it be Tehran, Turkey, Thailand or West Texas!*

As an integrally-informed leader, you must understand that in Traditional cultures, both Modern and Postmodern values tend to be viewed not only with skepticism and suspicion, but often with fear and in some cases, hatred.

Fear is a major motivator underlying a feeling of "us vs. them" in the form of a common enemy that threatens the Traditional way of life of the Traditional lifestyle (which is viewed as the "natural order of things" and defined by the higher authority (the Bible, the Koran or the Communist Party).

> *Proponents of the Traditional worldview understand the fears and the motivations of Traditional readers and voters. They often use positional or perceived "moral authority" to galvanize loyalty and motivate followers and voters, or perhaps to gain views and viewers or sell books, as we see with profit-driven enterprises such as Fox News and many of the publishers of the ubiquitous right-wing propaganda streaming into Traditional homes worldwide. These practices have recently become more widely known as a result of the defamation lawsuit that Dominion Voting Systems brought against Fox News.*

If you aren't familiar with this, I will summarize it briefly here. In 2021, Dominion filed a defamation suit against Fox News for the extensive false claims the network pushed after the 2020 U.S. election.

Fox News questioned the results of the election and pushed false conspiracy theories more than 800 times in the weeks following the election. Fox News executives knowingly promoted the "Big Lie" as it is now known.

Of course, this Traditional worldview is not just on television. I live in the U.S. so will use some examples from my part of the world. Books such as Sean Hannity's *Deliver Us from Evil* and Bill O'Reilly's *Culture Warrior* make a convincing case that Modern and Postmodern values are a dangerous threat to the traditional way of life. So do Ann Coulter's books and Tucker Carlson's talk show episodes.

These are all useful examples of the fear and hatred of the other worldviews that that are seen to deviate from the "natural order" and the "one true way to think and behave."

It should be obvious that this Traditional mindset is based on a "parental orientation" to reality that is dualistic and binary. There are "parents" and "children" and not much in between.

The leader is seen as sort of a "parental" type figure. The followers are in the position of "children" who should obey the authority. The leader is the authority. This is why in leadership theory, this approach is usually referred to as "authoritarian" leadership.

For the Traditional worker, the authority (who is in the position of parent) is expected to tell the followers (who are in the position of children) how to work, how to succeed, how to be moral, and generally how to live a good life according to "God's plan" or according to the "one true way".

> *To an individual who holds this Traditional worldview, the person that has been anointed, appointed or elected is the de facto leader. People with a traditional mindset view leadership as "positional." So the "Minister" and the "Mayor" are the defacto leaders. But there is one very important exception to this principle. If the appointed or elected person does not share their traditional values and beliefs, then they will be aggressively discredited and rejected as illegitimate, a fake or a fraud.*

This is very important to understand. In this scenario where the leader is discovered or revealed to not actually possess traditional values or beliefs, that elected leader is is then quickly viewed as *illegitimate, a fake, a fraud, or an opportunist* who is only doing it for egocentric or economic gain, and should be removed from that position as quickly as possible, in some cases, by any means necessary!

This reliably explains and predicts the right-wing behavior toward elected leaders viewed as "liberals." Perhaps there is no better example of this than how the United States traditional values voters reacted to the election of Barack Obama. They (with rare exceptions) despised him, because they fear and often hate leaders that do not share their traditional values and beliefs. We saw this again when Joe Biden was elected as U.S. president.

Note that I said "that they believe" follow their traditional values. Unfortunately, it is not difficult for actual opportunists (a.k.a. "autocrats") who do not actually have traditional beliefs to convince gullible traditional voters that they do share their traditional beliefs in order to win their support or their votes.

This is why it is very common for traditional voters to vote against their own best interests and to elect politicians who are actually just manipulating them. This is the precise business model of Fox News and the U.S. Republican party for more than two decades: *rich people convincing poor people that the progressive people are trying to steal their freedom, their guns, and their way of life.* It is a very effective strategy. And yes, they know exactly what they are doing. This is a well-documented fact.

Following, I will share some profiles of stereotypical traditional mindset followers. I'm sure you will recognize one or all three of these profiles as employees, colleagues, or perhaps members of your family. Try to look for those patterns.

Once you learn to recognize these mindsets in others, you will know exactly which of the four universal leadership styles they will find resonant, will trust and will willingly follow and for whom they will offer their discretionary effort. Recall earlier, I said that if you use the wrong leadership style with the wrong follower, they will not see you as credible, worse, they may see you as clueless or even foolish.

Here is a real-life example of that principle in action.

If you use a Humanistic leadership style with one of these people, it will destroy your credibility in their eyes. They will see you as just "not getting it" (that is you don't get how the world really is). And they may see you as clueless, or even foolish. So as you read about John, Susan and Daniel on the following pages, use this opportunity to find your followers in these descriptions!

John - True Believer

It's true, I've been called "straight laced" more than once. But people who know the Truth have a duty to defend it, even if it means being politically incorrect. People talk about "shades of gray" but as far as I'm concerned, right is right and wrong is wrong. Ultimately, almost everything is black and white, and those who suggest otherwise are just avoiding moral responsibility.

Susan - School Counselor

I love God, my family, and my country—in that order. I'm particularly proud of my nationality—when I hear people criticizing the leaders of my country I tend to feel rather insulted and often angry. I really feel that some things are simply not ours to question, and that obedience and loyalty are the highest virtues to which a person can aspire for. I work as a school counselor. I'm sometimes baffled why so many of today's kids go to such great lengths to be "different." By striving to be such "non-conformists" they don't fit in. Also, I feel frustrated by our school's tolerance for modes of dress and conduct that I find socially unacceptable and are against the family values that all schools should reinforce.

Daniel - Faith-Based Counselor

I teach a vocational rehab class for single parents and one of the things I stress to my students is that if you follow the rules—both in my class and life in general— you're bound to come out all right. With the world as unpredictable as it is, it just doesn't pay to take many risks or deviate from what's been proven to work. What is most important is having stability and knowing that you and those you love will have a secure future.

Authority Leadership

People with the Traditional mindset only willingly follow leaders who they see as having positional or moral authority, and who share their traditional beliefs. Therefore, they tend to follow leaders who are perceived as having that positional or moral authority, and who use that authority to prescribe the "one right way."

In other words, people with traditional mindsets see the "Authority leader," as the most credible, legitimate and trustworthy leaders. This term, "authoritarian leadership," is the accurate, widely-acknowledged academic term for this authority-centric style of leadership. For corporate audiences, especially ones that are composed of a lot of traditionalists, the term "Authority" or "Bureaucratic" leadership is preferred.

In this leadership style, the person with positional authority leads via chain of command.

> *This approach is "Hierarchical" and is characterized by compliance with the rules to meet the requirements dictated by the person with authority. While fear and guilt are primary motivators for followers with this Traditional mindset, they do not want their leaders to show either of these emotions. Effective authoritarian know this and rarely, if ever, admit fear, or that they don't know something or that they have made a mistake.*

That kind of "vulnerability based self-disclosure works well with Humanistic leadership with followers with an Affiliative mindset, but "authority leaders" (leading Traditional followers) rarely if ever admit their mistakes, their lack of knowledge or their fears, doubts or uncertainties. George W. Bush, a well-known authority-style leader, understood this implicitly. In his eight years as President of the United States, even in the face of incontrovertible evidence of poor judgment and costly errors (financial, military, international affairs, many millions of unnecessary deaths and so on), he never admitted making a single mistake.

While many have criticized this behavior, to his credit, this was exactly what his large base of "traditional values voters" wanted to see in their leader.

People with other mindsets tend to view this kind of behavior as an inability to admit mistakes or learn from them, yet people with this Traditional mindset will describe this same behavior as "principled."

This Traditional mindset is seen in popular leadership authors and theorists write books about the innate "character traits of leaders," the enduring "laws of leadership," or the "steps to being a great leader." Author John Maxwell's bestselling books are excellent examples of the traditional view of leadership. While Modern and Postmodern writers criticize what they consider to be reductionist approaches to life and leadership, it is very important to remember that advocates of this worldview (such Tucker Carlson, Glenn Beck, Sean Hannity, Ann Coulter) are so popular precisely because a large percentage of the population (estimated 40% in the U.S.) have adopted this Traditional worldview.

Integrally-informed leadership is concerned with seeing the world as it actually is and meeting people in it as they actually are. Integrally-informed leaders realize that although the Authority (Bureaucratic) leadership style may lack a certain nuance as compared to other styles, it is exactly the approach that a very large percentage of the population is most resonant with.

Power Mindset

Previously, I used the word "Imperial" to describe this worldview. As mentioned previously, worldviews are a psychological and somewhat academic term. For corporate audiences, we often pivot to "mindset" terminologies to offer a more user-friendly vernacular.

Here, when describing people who hold this worldview, I will introduce a new term, the "Power-Centric Mindset" or "Power Mindset" for short People with a Power mindset identify with being strong, courageous risk takers, who are capable of defending themselves in a dangerous world and getting what they want, when they want it. They emphasize personal power as defined by the ability to live outside conventional rules and gratify their desires. They value power, protection, freedom, respect, and control. Most importantly, they prefer to follow leaders who are perceived as being the strongest, toughest, and most dominant; in other words, leaders who use an Autocratic Leadership style.

Seeing the World Through a Power-Centric Lens

Academics refer to this worldview as the "Imperial worldview". It's easy to see this worldview dominating many periods of human history. You have probably heard it described as "Machiavellian." This term derives from the book The Prince written in 1513 by Niccolo Machiavelli as a pragmatic guide to getting and keeping power in a dangerous world. In The Prince, Machiavelli famously advocates "the ends justify the means." This pretty much sums up the Imperial worldview and the Autocratic Leadership style that is best paired with it.

When you look at the world through this Power-centric lens, you see a jungle filled with predators and selfcentered people, where only the strongest and most cunning survive and thrive. If this is your world, or at least your worldview, you tend to view others as competitors for scarce resources and will tend to interpret hesitation, softness, or even kindness, as signs of weakness. From this point of view, team members are useful allies in the on-going quest for power and when a common enemy is identified, the team can marshal its resources quite effectively.

> *To this worldview, "might" really does make "right." The "haves" deserve their status and privilege because they are powerful and dominant, and the "have not's" deserve their status because of their weakness or incompetence. Above all, people with the Power mindset demand respect and will respond favorably only to those capable of commanding it.*

Empirical Research

My descriptions in this book are all based on empirical research out of Harvard, Yale, Boston College, Washington University and other top institutions. For this short book, I will mention the academic terms that the different leading psychologists use for this worldview / follower mindset. Kegan uses the term "Imperial," McClelland uses "Power," Wade uses "Egocentric," Graves uses "Egocentric-Exploitive, "Loevinger uses "Self-Protective," Kohlberg uses "Self-Interest" and Torbert uses "Opportunist." When I'm using "follower mindset" terminology, I say "Power" mindset and when I'm using the worldview term, drawing from Kegan, I say "Imperial" worldview. Although I don't use Wilber's color schemes in this book written for a mainstream audience, for my readers who are students of Integral theory, I will mention here that the Wilberian color code for this worldview is "red."

Understanding People With a Power Mindset

People who identify with the Power mindset tend to be persuasive, egocentric, courageous, impulsive, and often charismatic. People with this mindset play crucial roles in society: the need for people who possess great courage and inner strength and are willing to take enormous risks.

However, people with this mindset are not always appreciated, because they also tend to be fiercely independent—"I live by my rules alone" and are disinterested in conforming to the status quo (including many societal norms).

They have a tendency to think mainly of themselves and can be insensitive to others' needs and desires in their own uncompromising push to break free from limits, satisfy their desires, or impose their will.

> *Some people confuse the Power mindset with the Achiever mindset. Although both the Power and Achiever mindsets are driven to "win" or "dominate", the "Achiever" drive is fueled by excellence, competitiveness and status, while the Power mindset is motivated by power, respect and glory.*

The Imperial worldview (and Power mindset) can be found in every socioeconomic system, but may be more readily noticeable in inner cities and in isolated rural areas. It is common to encounter people with this mindset in tough environments such as reform schools, heavy construction, oil and gas refineries, and prisons. These are the life conditions that give rise to and reward Power mindsets. Oftentimes people with a Power mindset were raised in or spent many years in these life conditions. When they move on to new circumstances they may carry that worldview with them. As you would expect, people with this mindset gravitate toward social groups that value toughness, aggression, and physical prowess and that encourage behavior sometimes considered "beneath social norms."

Following are profiles of people with a Power mindset. As with the other profiles I have provided in this book, please use these as archetypes and think about how these profiles remind you of some of the people in your life, or perhaps former bosses or co-workers.

> *People with this Power mindset do not respond well to "Strategic," "Humanistic," or "Authority" styles of leadership. They do not respect leaders who use those approaches. People with the Power mindset only respect Autocratic leadership.*

So, it is important that you recognize this mindset by seeing the patterns that I am providing you in these profiles.

Mike - Bouncer

I grew up in a tougher part of town—maybe that explains why I've always felt most comfortable in situations where it's "do or die." I did well in school but was bored with it. I dropped out of college and worked as a bouncer for a few years. I enjoyed it but I wanted to make money, so I parlayed my intellect, instinct, and charisma into a successful career in mergers and acquisitions. It's a ruthless business well-suited for me—I was never shy about drawing blood. I work hard and play hard. I generally stay out of trouble though I have had a few close calls. Ask my friends and they'll tell you there's never a dull moment.

Jill - Conservative Talk Radio Host

I've hosted my own radio show for about five years now. It's a tough gig, but fortunately, I enjoy a game of hardball. Though I'm charismatic, I'm known for going for the jugular and being able to verbally dominate a caller, even if their argument is better than mine. Basically, I operate on the premise that if somebody's not strong enough to hold their own with me, they don't deserve much respect.

Sheila - Server

I learned a long time ago that power leads to getting what you want, and that a woman with sex appeal has power over most men. Today, I'm a waitress in one of the most exclusive clubs in town. I basically make a killing by pouring on the nice and, when necessary, flashing a bit of skin. But it's not just about the money, I like the feeling that I'm in control. And I like working in an atmosphere where people aren't concerned about anything but having a good time.

Autocratic Leadership

People like Sheila, Mike and Jill with this Power-centric mindset only willingly follow leaders who they respect, and they do not respect weakness. Therefore, they tend to follow leaders who are perceived as having the most power, in other words, leaders who use an Autocratic Leadership style.

Autocratic leaders are motivated by power and respect, not by "people skills." The Autocratic approach to leadership is "Unilateral" and can be summed up as follows: *impose one's will through reputation, fear and respect, tightly control information and choices, reward compliance and punish disloyalty.*

Try to recall how the world appears through the lens of an Imperial worldview. If you perceive the world as a jungle or battlefield, then you are likely to believe the best way to advance toward your goals is always to protect yourself, gain power, and outmaneuver others who are perceived as either obedient loyalists or as obstacles, enemies or threats. Note that for autocratic leaders, both the obedient loyalists and the enemies are seen as objects to be manipulated.

If you read any of the books written by former Donald Trump employees about the man you will discover a textbook-accurate description of this Autocratic leadership style. As mentioned in an earlier chapter, bookstores are filled with popular titles that advocate this Autocratic leadership style. As I mentioned, these numerous books would not be so popular if there wasn't a market for them. I will remind you of the Stanly Bing books: *What Would Machiavelli Do? The Ends Justify the Meanness and Sun Tzu Was a Sissy: Conquer Your Enemies, Promote Your Friends, and Wage the Real Art of War* and the Robert Greene books *The 48 Laws of Power* and *The 50th Law*. Greene writes, "Learning the game of power requires a certain way of looking at the world, a shifting of perspective." From this autocratic perspective, everyone wants power and everyone is in a constant duplicitous game to gain more power at the expense of others.

While this autocratic style can be extremely useful on the battlefield or the oil field, unfortunately, this style has been seen on the rise even in modern countries, even in prominent leadership roles in government.

Many books (and studies) are available that provide a detailed account of the advantages and (huge) disadvantages seen when this style of leadership is deployed outside of the battlefield or oil field. Much carnage ensues. Another excellent resource for students of Autocratic leadership, especially when it is used in the wrong context, see Harvard's Barbara Kellerman's book, *The Enablers: How Team Trump Flunked the Pandemic and Failed America.*

The problem with this autocratic leadership approach is that people for whom the autocratic leadership style is their dominant style tend to be primarily or exclusively concerned with themselves and perhaps their immediate family or shareholders. Autocratic leadership simply does not work very well when those leaders have the responsibility of the wellbeing of a large diverse constituency of people whose welfare rely on wise decision-making that benefits the greater good.

However, we must never lose sight of the fact that people with a Power mindset, like Mike, Sheila and Jill in our profile examples, strongly prefer autocratic leaders.

We saw this in full effect in the United States at "Trump Rallies" in 2016-2020, and we see it anywhere a population of people with imperial worldviews feel unfairly treated and are looking for a "strongman" leader who promises to "defeat their enemies."

Most people reading this book do not have a primary Imperial worldview and therefore may find this Autocratic style of leadership unappealing, or even feel a strong aversion to it. But you must remember, everyone doesn't think like you do. Always remember that people with an Imperial worldview love autocratic leaders. In fact, they see Autocratic leadership as the only legitimate form of leadership.

Let's take a closer look at this and use our newfound "worldview lenses" to see how the other three mindsets view this Autocratic leadership style. People who primarily identify with the Affiliative mindset (the Postmodern worldview) find the Autocratic style appalling and think such leaders should not be allowed to lead; they should be stripped of power.

People who primarily identify with the Traditional mindset believe these "power-centric" folks have lost their way and need to be "saved." In their mind, what these "lost souls" need is Jesus (or Allah depending on the culture their parents raised them in). This "save the lost souls" mentality is the basis of popular traditional programs such as the "12-Step" recovery programs which are quite useful for power-centric and traditional addicts but really risky for people with modern and postmodern worldviews.

Some Traditionals do vote for autocrats if they believe the autocrats holds their same ethnocentric beliefs, and if they believe the autocrat's claims that he will defeat their enemies. We see this with right-wing "Nationalists" movements wherever they are found. (Many examples of this have been seen in recent years, not only in the United States but also in Europe, Australia and across Asia).

However, the moment that Traditionalists recognize that the self-serving, manipulative autocrat does not actually share their traditional beliefs, they then see the same leader as immoral, and one who should be stripped of power. To invoke our familiar example from recent American history, this was seen when a subset of right-wing Republicans and gullible evangelicals realized that they had been hoodwinked, and instantly transformed from red cap-wearing MAGA loyalists to "Never Trumpers."

What about Achievers? How do they view the Autocratic leadership style?

People who primarily identify with the Achiever mindset consider the Autocratic style to be a bit extreme, but a potentially useful tool for difficult employees or suppliers that won't respond to any other tactics. Understandably, many new students of integrally-informed approaches to leadership have difficulty imagining themselves using the Autocratic leadership style.

However, the truth is that people who primarily identify with the Power mindset are extremely unlikely to respond to the Strategic, Humanistic or Authority leadership styles. What do you do if you encounter, or manage, these Power-centric folks?

Integrally-informed leaders understand the importance of recognizing this mindset when they encounter it, and if necessary, drawing upon aspects of the Autocratic style (hopefully in judicial combination with other styles) to connect with, influence and motivate people who only respect this style.

In this chapter I have provided a brief introduction to my Leadership Rosetta Stone framework.

This is such an important topic, I wrote two books on the subject.

The first book looks at this topic through a slightly more "academic" lens. It is entitled *The Leadership Rosetta Stone: The Unifying Theory of Leadership That Deciphers 100 Years of Contradictory Theories and Reveals Which Leadership Approaches Will Work with Which People and Circumstances.*

The second book, which is the second book in this Universal Leadership Model series and is highly recommended, is entitled *Leadership Styles: How the Most Successful Leaders Adapt and Optimize Their Leadership Style to Maximize Their Influence and Impact.*

Next, I will offer specific benchmarks for "levels of proficiency" in each of the essential leadership abilities.

CHAPTER 7: EVALUATING LEADERSHIP ABILITY

In this chapter, I will go into more detail about the three essential abilities and nine skill sets that competent leaders are proficient in. Previously, I introduced the three inherent leadership responsibilities. In this chapter, I will expand on them to unpack the most common skill sets that leaders draw upon to fulfill those responsibilities. As mentioned earlier, "character traits" or vague "leadership qualities" can't be taught or learned in any reasonable amount of time. But technique (also known as behavior) can absolutely be trained and learned relatively quickly. This is the key to rapid leadership development. I'm going to be blunt again here. Please stop listening to bogus leadership advice from the leadership industry's "snake oil salesmen" who push vague concepts like EQ, confidence, trustworthiness, or charisma.

Vague concepts have never helped a leader increase this technical and complex skill. Seek advice from people who have legitimate expertise in the requisite leadership skills and "techniques" and know how to help clients develop those skills (by teaching the requisite techniques, not vague concepts).

"What, abandon EQ" you might be saying to yourself? No, of course you don't abandon your ability for emotional intelligence.

Of course, emotional intelligence is important—that is the capacity that we refer to when we use the term—along with *social intelligence, cognitive intelligence, moral intelligence,* and so on.

I realize this intelligence is important; in fact, I have taught and written extensively about these human capacities over the last two decades. My colleagues and I have developed assessments to measure low, medium and high levels of development along these bits of intelligence (which integral and developmental psychologists call "lines of development"). However, and this is the key point, in my 20+ years I've never ever, not even once, seen a person's EQ improve by lecturing them about what it is.

Stop talking about emotional intelligence. You are wasting your breath and the listener's time, attention and energy.

This is a somewhat nuanced but extremely important point I am making here.

This lies at the heart of what is wrong with the leadership development industry.

> *Talking about intelligence does nothing to increase it. This is akin to taking piano lessons and the instructor talks about the qualities of great piano players. The instructor goes on and on of the benefit of "musical intelligence."*

It is so obvious when we talk about other technical and complex skills (playing a musical instrument, learning to play a sport like baseball or basketball, or learning karate).

But when we talk about the technical and complex skill of leadership, people somehow miss the obvious fact that we are talking about a technical and complex skill made up of techniques and skills.

> *If you went to basketball camp, the instructors would not talk about "athletic intelligence" (kinesthetic intelligence). Rather, you would practice dribbling, passing, shooting and rebounding!*

The only time you should be talking about intelligences or "leadership traits" is when you are creating a profile for hiring. If you are in a hiring role, then yes, you want to screen and hire people with high EQ.

This book is about leadership development.

Emotional intelligence improves when and only when you give a person a specific technique, a practice, to adopt and use daily over many months.

This is the only way to improve these skills: through practice.

Most leadership training and coaching programs talk about "EQ" (and trust and culture and inclusivity and so on) as vague concepts and very few offer specific techniques as daily practices that actually grow these capacities.

This is the key distinction you must grasp to appreciate my this uniquely effective approach to eadership development.

If your objective is to improve your leadership skills rapidly, then you will want to put most of the emphasis on the specific skill sets you need to enhance the abilities you are targeting. We must come down out of the clouds of vague concepts into specific behaviors that can be memorized, practiced and matured with time (and with which we can layer on additional skills that comprise the complex abilities we associate with leadership).

Planning

You will recall that leaders articulate a vision (a direction) and suggest some kind of plan to achieve that vision. They also have to align stakeholders with values and purpose of the organization and cultivate their commitment to that vision or direction, and they must guide or "steer" the organization toward that vision over time. For simplicity's sake and to feel familiar to the widest population of book readers, I've gone with the single word "planning" here, but the word "steering" would be another one-word way to describe this responsibility.

A more nuanced name for this first dimension of leadership responsibility would be *"Strategy & Stakeholders."*

This is the subject of my book entitled *Strategy & Stakeholders: How the Most Successful Leaders Analyze Organizational Needs, Create Compelling Vision, Enroll and Align Stakeholders and Craft Smart, Evolving Strategic Plans.*

Teaming

You will recall that leaders "create the container" and "set the tone" of the relationships among the team members. The leader establishes some kind of structure for the team(s) including the norms that people are expected to follow in terms of supporting, relating, communicating and motivating. This may be explicitly communicated or simply be implicit (setting the example that others can follow). Think of this group of activities as the interpersonal dimension of leadership. I've used the word "teaming" here, but some readers may be more resonant with the word "relating."

A more nuanced name for this second dimension of leadership responsibility would be *"Teamwork & Culture."*

This is the subject of my book entitled *Teamwork & Culture: How the Most Successful Leaders Set People Up for Success, Cultivate High Performance Teamwork and Leverage Communication Versatility to Keep Everyone Engaged and Motivated.*

Executing

As we saw earlier, this area of leadership responsibility includes guiding productive work to execute the strategy (implement the plans), and manage people's performance and the projects they are working on. It is concerned with all of the activities an organization engages in, that have to do managing projects using the appropriate tools to coordinate work across teams, meeting expectations and being able to hold each other accountable to tasks, milestones, and deadlines, and making sure that people are focused on the right things and staying productive, efficient and effective. Some people think of this as "operational leadership". You may have heard the term "boots on the ground." You might also think of this dimension as the "hands" and "feet" of leadership.

A more nuanced name for this third dimension of leadership responsibility would be *"Execution & Performance."*

This is the subject of my book entitled *Execution & Performance: How the Most Successful Leaders Close Employee Performance Gaps, Maintain Accountability and High Productivity, and Consistently Deliver Exceptional Results.*

In the next section, I will pass across these three again, this time making them more nuanced as leadership literature would describe them, and offer a more detailed description of many of the "activities" and specific practices that leaders engage in order to fulfill these responsibilities. This convention of "activities" will become extremely important. As mentioned before, stories of great leaders and descriptions of leaders' personality traits do little (if anything) to help you become a better leader. But if you understand the activities that effective leaders do, and you learn the specific techniques (behaviors) they leverage to complete those activities successfully, then you can rapidly improve your leadership ability.

Clearly there are a lot of leadership activities and practices that fall into these three groupings. These three abilities are comprised of skill sets, and the skill sets are, in turn, comprised of about half a dozen discrete skills (methods or techniques that have been internalized to the point that they are instinctual). If you survey the literature on leadership, you would find dozens of discrete techniques, tactics or skills related to each of these three fundamental categories.

While there is an infinite number of techniques, methods and skills for each of these skill sets, we have found, applying Pareto's law, that it boils down to only about half a dozen specific leadership techniques / skills that matter most (for each of the nine skill sets).

This process is related to "Complex Skill Instructional Design" we discussed in an earlier chapter. This is how we learn to play baseball (throwing, catching, batting, running) or to play a musical instrument (playing notes, combining notes into chords, musical theory of keys and chord progressions, and combining these elements into songs). To repeat, it is impossible to learn a complex skill (sports, martial arts, playing an instrument, flying an airplane or leadership) without breaking the complex skill down into its component parts, and then learning the technique that supports each of those skills.

Think of it this way. You and every leader you have ever worked with (or for) has drawn on these skill sets (by whatever name) to fulfill their leadership responsibilities.

You may be wondering about level of skill, or level of competency. You are right to recognize that natural talent in each of these skill set areas is not evenly distributed across the population. While all leaders engage in some version of these activities which are inherent to leadership, some are very skillful and others have not had the benefit of training and mentorship, and others may not have strong natural instincts in that area.

For example, every leader "motivates" their followers in one way or another without exception.

Similarly, even if a leader does not have any natural ability or formal training in "planning," they still make plans in some way, even if those plans are very rudimentary. Even an unsophisticated leader would say, "This is my plan."

A final example is communication. Without exception, all leaders draw upon whatever communication skills they have to coordinate efforts.

It bears repeating that these three inherent leadership responsibilities and nine skill sets are universal. Talent, training and competency level are not universal. Some of the leaders you worked with (and for) may have been terrible at communication, motivation, planning and so on. But if they were in a leadership role for long, they were in fact doing some version of the activities that fall into that "bucket" we call "communication," "motivation," and "planning."

I will define exactly what competency looks like at lower, intermediate and higher levels of proficiency and each of these skill set areas in this book (along with best practices and high-leverage methods to rapidly elevate those skills). But let's not get ahead of ourselves. For now, it is helpful to just recognize the fact that these nine skill sets are fundamental to leadership and, in turn, organizational life.

You are already doing these nine things. All leaders (who are competent enough to stay in a leadership role for very long) do some versions of these nine activities in order to fulfill their responsibilities. With all of that in mind, let's dive in to the details now.

The Strategy & Stakeholder Practices

In our first pass, I called this area of responsibility simply "Planning." I will now introduce the more nuanced term, *Strategy & Stakeholders.*

You will recall that I defined this area of responsibility as: establishing vision and goals, crafting strategy and plans, and enrolling stakeholder commitment.

Strategy & Stakeholders includes all of the activities related to: establishing and communicating the purpose, vision, and values of the organization, making sense of what is happening in the current environment including evaluating relevant challenges and opportunities, strategic thinking, prioritizing strategic objectives, crafting strategic plans, and enrolling stakeholder commitment in the organizational vision and the strategy to achieve shared goals.

As mentioned previously, because these skill sets are fundamental and universal, you should be able to recognize the activities in each "bucket" because they are activities that you and every other leader does in one way or another (perhaps by a different name). As we unpack each skill set in later chapters, we will weave in leadership best practices which are the behaviors that skillful leaders engage when drawing upon this skill set to fulfill their leadership responsibilities.

As the saying goes, "repetition is the mother of skill." I am sure you are aware of the benefit of revisiting and reviewing key concepts, especially, as we layer in additional distinctions. I will use this convention often in this book by re-introducing previous concepts and adding another layer of nuance. As we make a second pass over these core competencies, I will replace the simple, commonly used terms introduced previously with my more nuanced terms.

Sensemaking

This skill set is concerned with your ability to evaluate the landscape (both external conditions as well as internal organizational dynamics) to determine what

is really happening, the key drivers impacting the environment, what is most important for your organization, and what is most needed.

Stakeholder Alignment

This skill set is concerned with your ability to establish and articulate your organization's direction in the form of vision, values and purpose, then to align all key stakeholders so that they feel and demonstrate a shared commitment to it.

Dynamic Steering

This skill set is concerned with your ability to develop and evolve organizational strategies, establish and revise goals and objectives, and prioritize the highest-leverage projects that will lead to desired outcomes each quarter and each year.

The Teamwork & Culture Practices

In our first pass, I called this area of responsibility and this "essential ability" simply "Teaming." I will now introduce a more nuanced term, "Teamwork & Culture."

I define this area of responsibility as: Setting your team(s) up for success with the appropriate structure and culture, and supporting and communicating with them to keep them optimally engaged and motivated.

Teamwork & Culture includes all of the activities related to setting your people up for success, creating and maintaining a conducive environment including a healthy culture and emotional climate, and keeping people engaged and motivated using appropriate and effective communication, including feedback, listening, collaboration, and managing conflict

Next, I will very briefly introduce each of the three skill sets that leaders draw upon to fulfill their responsibilities associated with this dimension. And I will replace the commonly-used terms, with more nuanced names.

Creating the Container

This skill set is concerned with your ability to set people up for success—this includes equipping teams with the structure, culture, training, tools and support they need to achieve shared organizational goals.

Conscious Communication

This skill set is concerned with effective communication which involves social awareness, listening, framing, feedback, dialog, collaboration, working with assumptions and interpretations, and managing conflict.

Meaningful Motivation

This skill set is concerned with keeping people engaged and motivated by understanding their needs, values, and intrinsic motivators, and appealing to each person's particular worldview and leadership preferences.

The Execution & Performance Practices

In our first pass, I called this area of responsibility and this "essential ability" simply "Executing." I will now introduce a more nuanced term, *"Execution & Performance."*

For review, I defined this area of responsibility as: guiding productive work to execute the strategy, coordinating work, implementing projects, and managing people's performance.

Execution & Performance, includes all of the activities related to establishing roles and responsibilities, identifying and closing performance gaps, planning and managing projects using the appropriate tools to coordinate work across teams, and maintaining high productivity so that the organizational resources are used efficiently to achieve shared goals in the desired time frames. There are three practices leaders use to fulfill this area of responsibility. They are as follows...

Performance Management

This skill set involves managing performance so that responsibilities, expectations, and agreements are consistently met, including ongoing "accountability conversations" to manage commitments and breakdowns when expectations are not met.

Project Implementation

This skill set is concerned with planning quarterly and monthly projects, defining objectives, workstreams, tasks and timelines, and coordinating the people and activities necessary to stay on track and consistently complete projects on time and on budget.

Improving Productivity

The last skill set is concerned with your ability to help your organization complete work in a productive, organized, efficient and effective way, including managing calendars and tasks, running effective meetings, and staying focused and proactive in the face of distractions, urgencies and obstacles.

Now that we have established a high-level understanding of the nine skill sets that leaders draw upon (at whatever level of ability they currently possess) to fulfill their responsibilities, we can take bold steps toward our goal of rapidly increasing your leadership competency.

To draw again on my previously-used baseball analogy, soon we will enter the "batting cage" to work on our ability to hit the ball. But we have one more important foundation to lay that is necessary for success with an accelerating learning effort. But first, will take a close look at the four universal "follower mindsets" that unequivocally dictate which style of leadership a person will find credible, resonant and will want to follow.

Strategy & Stakeholders

As you will recall, *Strategy & Stakeholders* includes all of the activities related to establishing and communicating the purpose, vision, and values of the organization, making sense of what is happening in the current environment including evaluating relevant challenges and opportunities, strategic thinking, prioritizing strategic objectives, crafting strategic plans, and enrolling stakeholder commitment in the organizational vision and the strategy to achieve shared goals. It is helpful to orient our thinking about this dimension of leadership by reviewing some of the key questions, challenges and goals that leaders have when addressing this area of leadership.

Common Strategy & Stakeholder Questions

Following are some of the common questions leaders ask about this essential ability:

- What is the best way to make sense of our organizational landscape so that we can identify the best solutions for our challenges and opportunities?

- What is the best way to clarify our organization's vision and mission and engage all of our key stakeholders for maximum alignment and commitment?

- How should we develop our organizational goals, strategies and plans, prioritize the highest-leverage projects and communicate them to our teams effectively?

Common Strategy & Stakeholder Challenges

Following are some of the common challenges leaders report about this essential ability:

- Inadequate or weak sensemaking (analysis) leading to weak business strategies or bad decisions
- Need for the organization to pivot (but there is inertia and inadequate cooperation to make the shift)
- Stakeholders are not aligned and not bought in, stakeholder incentives are misaligned or in conflict
- Uncertainty (and fear) about the future, lack of agreement about what the organization should do
- Rapidly changing environment, uncertain environment (VUCA: volatility, uncertainty, complexity, ambiguity)
- The annual planning cycle is too slow, rigid, inefficient and outdated within a quarter or two
- Strategic planning tied to a budget rather than strategic organizational priorities
- The need to re-organize (execute a re-org) but there are numerous obstacles to overcome

Common Strategy & Stakeholder Goals

Following are some of the common goals leaders have regarding this essential ability:

- Do a better job of shared sensemaking, working together to analyze challenges (and opportunities)
- Increase ability to understand what is really happening and what is needed

- Find ways to strengthen strategic thinking skills for leaders, managers and teams
- More leverage, more focus, better at prioritizing opportunities, objectives, initiatives and projects
- Elevate team (organization's) strategic planning to-ols, skills and methods (better plans, more buy-in)
- Align/enroll stakeholders with organization's vision and strategy (for greater commitment and cooperation)

You are no doubt familiar with the "gap analysis." If we want to improve ability, we need to have some kind of reliable measurement or benchmark to compare against and to use to develop training methods, content and evaluate progress over time.

To my knowledge, reliable proficiency benchmarks for the main areas of leadership responsibility as well as the essential leadership skills (for each), are not available anywhere beyond this book.

There are some rudimentary assessments available that I don't find adequate. There are also some very sophisticated 360 tools for evaluating leadership psychology that requires significant training and an expensive certification to decipher which can be valuable but are not something that individual leaders (such as the readers of this book) can self-administer.

To address an important yet unmet need, I developed the benchmarks in this book drawn from more than 20,000 hours of experience researching, developing, evaluating, and training thousands of leaders over the last two decades.

We can view this capacity through the organizational lens and the individual leader lens. When we look through the former, we see a team and/or organizational capacity to address these concerns.

When we look through the latter, we see a leader's proficiency or competency in the skills that we associate with this dimension.

The below benchmarks are worded to use when evaluating a team or organization's current capability in this dimension, which reflects the leader's ability. These benchmarks are also helpful to use when asking members of a team to self-assess the team's current capability. Not only does this provide valuable insights to the leaders, it also is a terrific conversation starter that you can use to discuss this aspect of the team (or department or organization's) strengths and gaps which could be elevated to support the group's ability to achieve its shared objectives.

I introduced the low/medium/high levels of proficiency for each of the three essential abilities in Chapter 4: Leadership Abilities and Competencies. I will review those benchmark descriptions and supplement them with a description of how an executive describes what its like to function at that level of proficiency. Hopefully, this will help you discern where you and your team fall on the spectrum from low to high proficiency.

Lower Range

If your organization is in the lower range of proficiency in this ability, planning might feel reactive. There's little clarity around vision, few written plans, and low stakeholder commitment. A leader functioning in the lower range of this ability might describe it this way:

I wouldn't say that situational analysis, strategic thinking or stakeholder commitment is strong in our organization. We rely on our gut to evaluate current circumstances and decide what strategies we should deploy. We don't have strong written plans for the year or quarter. Our "organizational vision" is not clearly articulated. The level of cooperation and commitment of our stakeholders is on the lower side.

Intermediate Range

In the intermediate range of proficiency in this ability, you've made progress. You have plans, and your vision is articulated, but you might struggle with deeper stakeholder buy-in or dynamic connections between strategies and execution. A leader functioning in the intermediate range of this ability might describe it this way:

We do put some effort into trying to understand the "core drivers" impacting us before we attempt to craft a strategy and make plans. We have written annual and quarterly plans. We have articulated our organizational vision statement (or mission). We need to do a better job of enrolling our stakeholders and getting their buy-in and commitment.

Higher Range

At the higher range of proficiency in this ability, planning feels like a well-oiled machine. Vision, strategy, and stakeholder commitment are seamlessly integrated. Your organization is not just reacting—it's proactively shaping its future. A leader functioning in the higher range of this ability might describe it this way:

Our organization is great at "vision," "strategic thinking and planning" and achieving "shared stakeholder commitment." Some of our leaders brought in tools that help us discern key drivers and root causes to use to craft high-leverage strategies. Our annual initiatives and quarterly objectives are dynamically linked to ongoing projects. We have well-articulated vision / mission / values statements and enjoy high levels of stakeholder commitment.

Benchmarking Teamwork & Culture Ability

Teamwork & Culture includes all of the activities related to setting your people up for success, creating and maintaining a conducive environment including a healthy culture and emotional climate, keeping people engaged and motivated using appropriate and effective communication, including feedback, listening, collaboration and managing conflict.

It is helpful to orient our thinking about this dimension of leadership by reviewing some of the key questions, challenges and goals that leaders have when addressing this area of leadership.

Teamwork & Culture Questions

Following are some of the common questions leaders ask about this essential ability:

- What are the best ways to set people up for success with the right kind of team structure and culture?
- How can we improve our feedback and performance reviews?
- How can we deal with people's assumptions and interpretations and avoid misunderstandings
- What are the best ways to keep people engaged and motivated especially with a diverse workforce?

Teamwork & Culture Challenges

Following are some of the common challenges leaders report about this essential ability:

- Low team or department morale (frustrated, discouraged, resentful)
- Low employee engagement or disengagement (low trust or toxic culture)

- Diversity / equity / inclusion issues
- How to manage remote workers and blended workforce (managing on Zoom)
- People are afraid to make mistakes or afraid to take initiative or take risks
- Reassuring workforce in difficult times that are intimidating, stressful or demoralizing
- Want to change culture but don't know how to shift to the desired culture
- Managers / leaders don't know how to motivate people
- Culture that emphasizes extrinsic motivators, fails to tap intrinsic motivation
- Difficulty motivating a diverse workforce, team members seem unmotivated, how to reach them?
- Guarded, defensive or ineffective communication (gaps in listening, dialog, collaboration skills)
- Not enough feedback, ineffective or unbalanced feedback
- Interpersonal or personality conflicts or team rivalries
- Change management, aligning process, messaging and cultural interventions with change

Teamwork & Culture Goals

Following are some of the common goals leaders have regarding this essential ability:

- Do a better job of setting up new team members for success (training, tools, structure)
- Get better at setting the right emotional tone for a positive and conducive working environment

- Getting better at motivating people and keeping morale high on teams
- We must get better at feedback (right way, right amount, in balance to keep people learning and motivated)
- More trust on our team(s) so we can have more honest and open dialog and more fruitful collaboration
- Get better at listening and dialog so we can improve our collaboration skills
- Do better working with assumptions and interpretations to avoid misunderstandings and conflict

Benchmarking

Below are the benchmarks to use when evaluating a leader, team or organization's current capability in this dimension. This not only provides valuable insights to leaders, but it also serves as a great conversation starter to discuss this aspect of the team's (or department's or organization's) strengths and gaps that could be elevated to support the group's shared objectives.

Lower Range

At the lower range of proficiency in this ability, teams struggle with communication, engagement, and trust. Motivation is low, and it's unclear how to build a culture that supports high performance. A leader and a team functioning in the lower range of proficiency in this skill set might describe it this way:

We need to do a better job of setting people up for success. While we have a few standout performers, the majority of our team members are disengaged or unmotivated. Communication skills are not our strong suit. It is unclear to me how to motivate this team to embrace high-performance teamwork.

Intermediate Range

At the intermediate range of proficiency in this ability, teams have decent trust and teamwork, but communication can still feel strained, and engagement isn't consistent across the board. There's a solid foundation, but room to grow. A leader and a team functioning in the middle range of proficiency in this skill set might describe it this way:

We enjoy a healthy culture and decent trust and teamwork. We would like to be better at motivating our team members and keeping people highly engaged. In terms of communication, some team members are good listeners, give effective feedback and know how to dialogue, but for others, communication often seems awkward or strained.

Higher Range

At the higher range of proficiency in this ability, communication, culture, and collaboration are strengths. Team members are motivated, engaged, and supported, and feedback and dialog flow effortlessly. A leader and a team functioning in the higher range of proficiency in this skill set might describe it this way:

Communication, teamwork and culture in general are our greatest strengths. Most of our people report that they feel well-equipped, well-trained, empowered and supported. Overall, our team members are highly motivated and engaged and we consistently practice effective communication in the areas of feedback, listening, dialog, collaboration, conflict management and so on.

Benchmarking Execution & Performance Ability

As you will recall, the *Execution & Performance* dimension includes all of the activities related to establishing roles and responsibilities, identifying and closing performance gaps, planning and managing projects using the appropriate tools to coordinate work across teams, and maintaining high productivity so that organizational resources are used efficiently to achieve shared goals in the desired time frames.

It is helpful to orient our thinking about this dimension of leadership by reviewing some of the key questions, challenges and goals that leaders have when addressing this area of leadership.

Common Execution & Performance Questions

Following are some of the common questions leaders ask about this essential ability:

- How can we hold people accountable and identify and close performance gaps so that expectations are consistently met?
- How can we coordinate the people and efforts (objectives, workstreams, timelines) so that our projects are consistently implemented successfully on time and on budget?
- How can we make sure work is completed in a productive, organized, focused, efficient and effective way (in challenging environments including working remotely often with lots of distractions and competing commitments)?

Common Execution & Performance Challenges

Following are some of the common challenges leaders report about this essential ability:

- Managers wearing too many hats / managers have "too much to do" with too little resources
- Leaders have multiple competing priorities and feel overwhelmed with unrealistic workload
- Lack of follow through or lack of accountability by individuals, teams or departments

- Unclear or poorly communicated expectations from boss therefore expectations often not met
- Department or organization is understaffed and lacks sufficient resources, we must do more with less
- Missing milestones and deadlines due to poor project management (or unrealistic expectations)
- Poor quality, sloppy work, disappointing results, unhappy customers
- Delegation not happening well or consistently (not clear, not realistic) and lack of follow through
- Difficulty with group decision-making, when decisions are made they are often met with resistance
- Managers lack the authority to make decisions necessary to achieve outcomes
- Confusion or lack of clarity about roles, responsibilities and who has what authority
- Inadequate project planning, projects are not well-defined, work streams lack clarity or accountability

Common Execution & Performance Goals

Following are some of the common goals leaders have regarding this essential ability:

- Clarify roles for all team members so people know what activities and outcomes are expected of them
- Help a team member who is struggling to close a performance gap
- Get better at holding people accountable, create a "culture of accountability"
- Get better at planning and managing projects using the appropriate tools to coordinate people and effort

- Assess and upgrade existing meetings, upgrade and enhance with current best practices
- Level up our time management practices to handle calendars and schedules better

Benchmarking

Below are benchmarks to use when evaluating a leader, team or organization's current capability in this dimension. These organizational benchmarks are very helpful to use when asking members of a team to self-assess the team's current capability. Not only does this provide valuable insights to the leaders, it also is a terrific conversation starter that you can use to discuss this aspect of the team (or department or organization's) strengths and gaps which could be elevated to support the group's ability to achieve its shared objectives.

Lower Range

At the lower range of proficiency in this ability, teams often struggle with accountability, time management, and project planning. Performance gaps go unaddressed, and productivity feels inconsistent at best. A leader and a team functioning in the lower range of proficiency in this skill set might describe it this way:

We have some obvious gaps in execution and accountability. Our team doesn't know much about time and task management. We hear complaints that meetings are viewed as ineffective. Our people manage their projects with simple tools such as post-it notes or spreadsheets (no shared dashboards or software being used). Beyond obligatory annual performance reviews, ongoing expectations, accountability and performance are rarely discussed openly.

Intermediate Range

At the intermediate range of proficiency in this ability, teams have started building execution skills. Some members use project management tools and strong productivity practices, but adoption is inconsistent. Accountability conversations happen, but they're often uncomfortable or infrequent. A leader and a team functioning in the middle range of proficiency in this skill set might describe it this way:

We execute sometimes, but we are inconsistent. Some team members have strong productivity skills; others don't. Some members have formal "project management" training and use dashboards to coordinate efforts, but the whole team has not adopted these tools. We try to make responsibilities and expectations explicit, but we don't do regular check-ins to identify and address performance gaps. Accountability conversations, when they happen, are often awkward.

Higher Range

At the higher range of proficiency in this ability, execution is a strength. Roles and responsibilities are clear, accountability is part of the culture, and project planning tools are widely used. Teams are focused, efficient, and rarely miss milestones. A leader and a team functioning in the higher range of proficiency in this skill set might describe it this way:

We really "execute" quite well. Most team members stay focused, efficient and productive. Several of our managers have prior project management experience and have helped us institutionalize disciplined project planning and follow-through habits (with shared dashboards, frequent check-ins and so on). Missed milestones are rare. We have clear responsibilities and expectations, and we are comfortable calling out and learning from the occasional "accountability breakdown."

Benchmarking the Nine Core Competencies

Next, I summarize the benchmarks for each of the three core competencies under each of the three abilities (planning, teaming, executing).

Strategy & Alignment

As you will recall, Strategy & Alignment, or simply "Planning" for short, is the essential leadership ability to envision a compelling future, align stakeholders with that vision, and dynamically guide the organization toward its objectives. This dimension requires leaders to make sense of complex environments, prioritize strategic goals, and chart a path forward.

Sensemaking

Description:

Leaders must analyze and interpret their internal and external environments to understand the key drivers of success and challenges. This involves asking critical questions, synthesizing diverse information, and discerning patterns that clarify the path forward. For example, during a market disruption, a leader using sensemaking would assess competitive shifts, customer trends, and internal capabilities to recalibrate strategies.

Benchmarks:

At the lower range, teams rely on quick, informal judgments to assess situations, often missing critical information and context.

At the intermediate range, teams discuss core drivers and key factors, but they lack structured tools or frameworks to ensure consistency and depth in their analysis.

At the higher range, leaders and teams consistently use advanced analytical tools and frameworks, incorporate diverse perspectives, and uncover root causes and key drivers, enabling precise decision-making and effective responses.

Strategic Alignment

Description:

Beyond articulating a vision, leaders must inspire commitment by aligning the interests, values, and priorities of stakeholders. Effective leaders use communication and negotiation to create a shared understanding of organizational goals. For instance, a leader launching a new initiative might align employees by demonstrating how their efforts contribute to both individual growth and collective success.

Benchmarks:

At the lower range of proficiency, leaders lack clear vision and alignment tools, resulting in disengaged stakeholders and inconsistent priorities.

At the intermediate range, leaders have some clarity on vision and goals but struggle with inconsistent alignment and buy-in from stakeholders.

At the higher range, leaders excel in crafting and communicating vision, enrolling stakeholders, and aligning efforts with strategic priorities, creating a cohesive and adaptable organization.

Organizational Steering

Description:

This skill set involves translating vision into actionable plans while remaining adaptive to changing circumstances. Leaders must set clear goals, monitor progress, and recalibrate strategies as needed. An example is a project leader revising timelines and reallocating resources when unexpected challenges arise, ensuring the team stays on course.

Benchmarks:

At the lower range of proficiency, organizations rely on static annual goals with minimal updates or alignment, often resulting in misaligned priorities and suboptimal performance.

At the intermediate range, organizations develop annual objectives and review them quarterly. However, gaps in prioritization and feedback loops lead to inconsistent alignment and execution.

At the higher range of proficiency, leaders employ dynamic, iterative planning processes. Priorities are continuously assessed, and high-leverage initiatives are aligned with organizational strategy, resulting in a highly adaptive and efficient system.

The Three Teamwork & Culture Competencies

As you will recall, Teamwork & Culture, or simply "Teaming" for short, reflects the leader's ability to cultivate an environment where individuals collaborate effectively, communicate openly, and feel motivated to contribute their best. This dimension shapes the relational and cultural fabric of the team or organization.

Creating the Container

Description:

Leaders must design the "container"—the organizational systems, team structures, and cultural norms that set the foundation for success. This involves clarifying roles, expectations, and processes. For instance, a leader of a newly formed team might establish clear operating principles and create opportunities for skill development to enhance team functionality.

Benchmarks:

At the lower range of proficiency, teams lack intentional structure or culture, often operating in silos. Team members feel unsupported, leading to disengagement and inconsistent performance.

At the intermediate range, some efforts have been made to establish structure and support systems, but gaps in culture or alignment result in missed opportunities for collaboration and growth.

At the higher range of proficiency, leaders create a dynamic, supportive environment where team members feel equipped, aligned, and motivated. Structures and culture are intentionally designed to support continuous improvement and high performance.

Communication

Description:

Relationships are central to teaming dimension of leadership and communication is the key to healthy relationships. Effective communication extends beyond information sharing. It includes active listening, managing conflicts, and fostering dialogue that deepens understanding. Leaders skilled in communication ensure that feedback is constructive, misunderstandings are resolved, and collaboration thrives.

Benchmarks:

At the lower range of proficiency, teams lack shared communication norms, resulting in frequent misunderstandings, unproductive conflict, and strained relationships.

At the intermediate range communication is moderately effective—some team members exhibit strong skills in listening and feedback, but there is no consistent application of best practices across the team.

At the higher range of proficiency, communication is intentional and impactful. Teams consistently frame messages, give and receive constructive feedback, and navigate conflicts in ways that strengthen relationships and improve outcomes.

Motivation

Description:

One of the more difficult things leaders are expected to do is to keep individuals engaged and maintain high morale on teams. Understanding what drives each team member is critical. Leaders must align intrinsic and extrinsic motivators, tailoring their approach to resonate with individual values and needs. For example, a manager might use personalized recognition to motivate an employee who values achievement while offering collaborative opportunities to someone who prioritizes connection.

Benchmarks:

At the lower range of proficiency, leaders struggle to engage their teams, relying heavily on generic extrinsic motivators. Morale and engagement are inconsistent, and performance suffers due to a lack of alignment with team members' values.

At the intermediate range, some efforts are made to understand and address motivators, but inconsistencies exist. Leaders may use limited tools and techniques, leading to variable engagement and occasional team frustration.

At the higher range of proficiency, leaders effectively align individual motivators with team and organizational goals. They understand and apply intrinsic and extrinsic motivators with precision, resulting in high engagement, alignment, and consistent achievement of objectives.

The Three Execution & Performance Competencies

Finally, we will look closely at the three core competencies seen in the execution dimension. As you will recall, Execution & Performance, or simply "Executing" for short, reflects the leader's ability to translate plans into tangible outcomes by managing people, projects, and performance. It ensures that organizational objectives are achieved efficiently and effectively, balancing short-term wins with long-term goals. This is the domain of team accountability and organizational productivity.

Performance Management

Description:

Effective leaders monitor, evaluate, and enhance team performance by setting clear expectations and holding individuals accountable. This involves regular check-ins, developmental coaching, and addressing underperformance constructively. For example, a manager might conduct quarterly performance reviews that include actionable feedback and development plans.

Benchmarks:

At the lower range of proficiency, teams struggle with clarity and execution due to informal processes and inconsistent accountability.

At the intermediate range of proficiency, some formal systems exist, but accountability and performance tracking remain inconsistent.

At the higher range of proficiency, teams exhibit disciplined planning, frequent feedback cycles, and effective follow-through, creating a culture of accountability and continuous improvement.

Implementation

Description:

Organizational leaders must coordinate complex projects, ensuring tasks are completed on time and within budget. This requires defining objectives, assigning responsibilities, and managing milestones. An example is a leader overseeing a product launch who ensures alignment across marketing, sales, and operations teams.

Benchmarks:

At the lower range of proficiency, teams use informal methods to manage projects, relying on basic tools like spreadsheets, resulting in frequent delays, unclear roles, and missed milestones.

At the intermediate range, some formal tools and methods are in place, but inconsistencies in application lead to variability in project outcomes. Teams may miss deadlines due to unclear responsibilities or inadequate tracking systems.

At the higher range, teams excel in disciplined project planning and execution. They use advanced tools, shared dashboards, and regular check-ins to ensure milestones are met, fostering a culture of accountability and efficient delivery.

Productivity

Description:

Sustained results depend on optimizing workflows, managing priorities, and overcoming obstacles. Leaders who excel in this area foster focus and efficiency, helping teams navigate competing demands. For instance, a leader might introduce a task management system to improve clarity and reduce bottlenecks.

Benchmarks:

At the lower range of proficiency, teams rely on informal processes, struggle with time and task management, and often find meetings inefficient and unproductive.

At the intermediate range, some tools and systems are in place, but inconsistencies lead to variable performance. Teams occasionally achieve focus and efficiency but are easily derailed by distractions and unclear priorities.

At the higher range of proficiency, teams consistently demonstrate high levels of organization and efficiency. Meetings are purpose-driven, tasks are tracked effectively, and distractions are minimized, resulting in sustained high performance.

This concludes the description of the low, intermediate and higher ranges of proficiency across the three "essential abilities of leadership" (planning, teaming, executing), and the nine core competencies of leadership (sensemaking, alignment, steering, creating the container, communication, motivation, performance management. I have kept these descriptions brief for purposes of this introductory book. I have written a whole book on each essential leadership ability, and I would like to encourage you to read those books for a deeper dive, with details of specific practices for each of the nine skill sets. If you want to refer to those books, I will list them below:

Strategy & Alignment: How the Most Successful Leaders Analyze Organizational Needs, Create Compelling Vision, Enroll and Align Stakeholders and Craft Smart, Evolving Strategic Plans

Teamwork & Culture: How the Most Successful Leaders Set People Up for Success, Cultivate High Performance Teamwork and Leverage Communication Versatility to Keep Everyone Engaged and Motivated

Execution & Performance: How the Most Successful Leaders Close Employee Performance Gaps, Maintain Accountability and High Productivity, and Consistently Deliver Exceptional Results

CHAPTER 8:
LEADERSHIP PRACTICES

In this chapter, I will introduce some of the most important techniques and specific leadership practices under each of the nine leadership core competencies (also called skill sets). I have written numerous books detailing the most important leadership techniques and practices. It is beyond the scope of this introductory book to teach you these practices, but I thought it would be helpful to give you an idea of the best practices that are useful for leaders to learn and use for each of the nine core competencies.

Leadership Practices in the Planning Dimension

Following are a few of the most common and most useful "best practices" that we see in the three skill sets that fall into the "Planning" ability of leadership.

Sensemaking Practices

1. Environmental Scanning: "Regularly analyze external trends to anticipate market shifts and risks."
2. Stakeholder Feedback: "Engage key stakeholders for insights into emerging challenges and opportunities."
3. Data-Driven Insights: "Leverage analytics to understand patterns and forecast outcomes."
4. Scenario Planning: "Develop possible future scenarios and their implications."
5. Competitor Benchmarking: "Continuously compare organizational practices against industry leaders."
6. SWOT Analysis: "Assess strengths, weaknesses, opportunities, and threats systematically."
7. Risk Assessment Workshops: "Collaborate with teams to identify and prioritize risks."
8. Cross-Functional Dialogues: "Encourage discussions across departments for diverse perspectives."
9. Emergent Trend Analysis: "Monitor macroeconomic and technological changes for strategic alignment."

Stakeholder Alignment Practices

1. Vision Cascading: "Translate the organizational vision into actionable objectives at every level."
2. Core Values Workshops: "Facilitate sessions to connect employees with the company's core values."
3. Consensus Building: "Foster agreement through structured discussions."
4. Stakeholder Mapping: "Identify and prioritize key influencers and decision-makers."

5. Organizational Storytelling: "Use compelling narratives to inspire alignment with strategic goals."
6. Regular All-Hands Meetings: "Update employees on progress and maintain engagement."
7. Values-Based Recognition: "Reward behaviors that reflect core organizational values."
8. Feedback Loops: "Establish mechanisms for two-way communication about alignment challenges."
9. Change Impact Analysis: "Assess and address the effects of strategic changes on stakeholders."

Organizational Steering Practices

1. Agile Goal Setting: "Adapt goals quarterly to reflect dynamic priorities."
2. OKRs (Objectives and Key Results): "Use OKRs to align teams and measure progress."
3. Strategic Pivot Meetings: "Regularly evaluate and shift resources to high-leverage opportunities."
4. Resource Optimization: "Continuously align budget, talent, and tools with strategic goals."
5. Progress Monitoring Dashboards: "Track performance metrics in real-time."
6. Quarterly Business Reviews: "Assess team and organizational progress periodically."
7. Scenario-Based Decision Making: "Prepare to adjust plans based on evolving conditions."
8. Contingency Planning: "Develop backup plans for critical initiatives."
9. Real-Time Adjustments: "Act on new data or developments without waiting for formal reviews."

Leadership Practices in the Teaming Dimension

Following are a few of the most common and most useful "best practices" that we see in the three skill sets that fall into the "Teaming" ability of leadership.

Creating the Container Practices

1. Team Charters: "Clearly define roles, responsibilities, and team norms."
2. Work Environment Design: "Optimize physical and digital workspaces for collaboration."
3. Structured Onboarding: "Provide comprehensive introductions to team norms and resources."
4. Shared Goal Setting: "Develop team goals collaboratively to foster ownership."
5. Competency Development: "Ensure continuous skill-building opportunities for all team members."
6. Team Accountability Systems: "Use transparent systems to track individual contributions."
7. Culture Mapping: "Regularly assess and adjust team culture for alignment with organizational values."
8. Cross-Functional Integration: "Facilitate collaboration across different teams."

Communication Practices

1. Active Listening: "Prioritize understanding others before responding."
2. Framing Techniques: "Craft messages tailored to audience values and context."
3. Structured Feedback Models: "Deliver feedback using clear, respectful frameworks."

4. Conflict Resolution Training: "Equip teams to address and resolve disagreements constructively."
5. Empathy Mapping: "Understand and address the emotional states of team members."
6. Inclusive Language: "Use communication that respects diversity and promotes equity."
7. Dialogue Practices: "Foster open-ended discussions to encourage collaboration."
8. Transparent Messaging: "Communicate intentions and decisions openly."
9. Nonverbal Communication Mastery: "Align body language with verbal messages."
10. Real-Time Clarifications: "Address misunderstandings immediately to avoid escalation."

Motivation Practices

1. Values Assessments: Understand the core values and the main motivational drivers of all of your employees manage them accordingly.
2. Interest-Centric Assignments: Align tasks with individual skills and interests.
3. Recognition Programs: Publicly celebrate individual and team achievements.
4. Intrinsic Reward Focus: Tie work to personal purpose and values.
5. Mentorship Opportunities: Facilitate mentoring to foster personal and professional growth.
6. Flexible Work Arrangements: Provide options to accommodate diverse employee needs.
7. Feedback and Appreciation: Deliver consistent and genuine positive feedback.

8. Career Pathing: Clarify opportunities for advancement within the organization.
9. Employee-Driven Initiatives: Encourage employees to lead projects they're passionate about.
10. Engagement Surveys: Regularly gather and act on employee sentiment data."

Leadership Practices in the Executing Dimension

Following are a few of the most common and most useful "best practices" that we see in the three skill sets that fall into the "executing" ability of leadership.

Performance Management Practices

1. Expectation Conversations: Make expectations explicit and reinforce them regularly.
2. Continuous Feedback Cycles: Shift from annual reviews to regular check-ins."
3. Accountability Conversations: Adopt methods to clarify and discuss commitments and cultivate a culture of accountability.
4. Performance Dashboards: Visualize key metrics for immediate insights."
5. Underperformance Action Plans: Develop strategies for addressing gaps.
6. Recognition of Effort: Acknowledge contributions, not just results.
7. Talent Reviews: Regularly assess and plan for team development.
8. Adaptive Performance Metrics: Revise criteria to align with evolving objectives.

9. 360-Degree Reviews: Gather feedback from peers, managers, and subordinates."

Implementation Practices

1. Project Planning: Make sure every project leader has answered the five project planning questions in writing (Why, What, How, When, Who)
2. Work Breakdown Structures (WBS): Break complex projects into manageable activities and tasks.
3. Gantt Charts: Visualize timelines and dependencies.
4. Agile Methodologies: Iteratively develop and adjust project outcomes.
5. Critical Path Analysis: Focus on activities that directly impact timelines.
6. Risk Mitigation Plans: Anticipate and address potential obstacles.
7. Cross-Functional Teams: Involve diverse expertise to enhance project outcomes.
8. Daily Standups: Hold brief check-ins to align efforts.
9. Project Close-Outs: Review lessons learned and celebrate successes.

Productivity Practices

1. Time Blocking: Allocate focused work periods on calendars."
2. Priority Matrices: Use tools like Eisenhower Matrix to prioritize tasks."
3. Focus Time Policies: Designate uninterrupted work periods.
4. Task Management Tools: Use platforms like Asana or Trello for coordination.

5. Personal Productivity: Teach techniques like scheduling appointments with yourself and staying focused using methods such as the Pomodoro technique.
6. Progress Checkpoints: Regularly review task completion rates.
7. Eliminating Bottlenecks: Address repetitive delays in workflows.
8. Workflow Automation: Leverage technology to reduce manual effort.

This concludes our brief summary of key practices effective leaders draw upon to maintain their effectiveness across the nine core competencies of leadership that underlie the three essential abilities of leadership. As mentioned previously, you can refer to my other 13 books for more detail on specific practices or considering taking a course or coaching program with me and my colleagues at Integral Leadership Academy.

CONCLUSION

Now that you have read this book, you have a strong familiarity with the Universal Leadership Model. You understand how there are four very different "paradigms" of leadership and each reflects a different set of assumptions about followers, organizations and the world in general. These parallel the four universal leadership styles. You also understand that a follower's worldview (based on their inherent assumptions about the world and the people in it) will determine very precisely what they seek in a credible, legitimate leader. To avoid the awkward situation of undermining your leadership credibility and appearing clueless or even foolish (in the eyes of your followers), you must adapt your leadership style to suit the needs and preferences of followers with different worldviews (and different ideas about what effective leadership is). You also learned the three inherent leadership responsibilities and the three "essential abilities" that all leaders everywhere use to fulfill those responsibilities. Finally, you gained clarity about how leaders must engage activities and draw upon skill sets (which we can also think of as core competencies) to fulfill their responsibilities. When we break it down into logical groupings, we see three "skill sets" for each of the three dimensions, for a total of nine skill sets. Naturally leaders in different contexts and cultures approach their responsibilities and express these skill sets based on their native style (or their versatile styles they have developed over the course of their career and their leadership education)

It is a significant accomplishment that you now know how leadership works universally. And you now understand that leadership is a technical and complex skill that is developmental in nature. While this is a significant achievement, knowledge is not the same as skill. A skill is a practice that has been engaged until it becomes a habit. As we discussed in the section on "deliberate practice," practice doesn't make perfect, rather, perfect practice makes perfect.

You cannot learn a technical or complex skill from a book. Complex skills are based on dozens of specific techniques that must all be learned, layered and combined, and practiced over time until they are internalized.

This book doesn't teach you the complex skill of leadership. But this book has revealed the most effective method to learn the complex skill of leadership.

You can't learn to play basketball or the guitar by just reading a book. Similarly, you can't learn the technical and complex skill of leadership from reading a book. But you can learn what you need to do in order to learn these techniques. I have the method introduced in this book (and detailed in several other books) for 25 years helping leaders adopt new skills rapidly with consistent results. You can get the same results if you engage the practices that I introduced in this book. I can't overstate this, facilitators and coaches must be experts in the specific techniques. You would never hire a guitar teacher or baseball coach who can't play guitar or who isn't a terrific baseball player. To break it down further into the techniques, you wouldn't go into a baseball "batting cage" to train that skill with someone who is a mindset coach or life coach who has never swung a bat (much less having expert-level proficiency).

To increase your competency in these skill sets you have learned about, you must practice the techniques for many weeks (or months). This is the only way to learn a complex skill. To put this method into practice, active and ongoing training in the specific techniques is required. That is best done in a training and/or coaching environment. We offer numerous training and coaching programs in various formats and at various price points to be able to accommodate most leaders in most circumstances.

This book provides the overview of the model that is the foundation of the leadership development work my team and I do every day, and it is also the basis of many leadership training and coaching programs that many other academies and institutes (and coaching programs) teach.

If you are serious about becoming a more effective leader, or if you support leaders (as a trainer or coach), I hope that you will pick up and read one or more of my other (longer, more detailed) books on this subject. You can find all of my books on Amazon.com.

I also hope you will consider joining one of the many Integral Leadership training and coaching programs that my partners and I offer. My fourteen books are used as textbooks at multiple institutions and academies and offer various versions of my Integral Leadership training by several different names, including the Integral Leadership Program (many versions across several academies), the Integral Leadership MBA, the Executive Leadership Program and the C-Suite Leadership Program. When you participate in an in-depth online or in-person training based on this content, and especially if you obtain group or one-on-one coaching from a coach who has been trained in my content, then you will be able to rapidly accelerate your development as a leader, and ultimately become the kind of respected influential, impactful, successful leader you know that you are destined to be.

I look forward to continuing this "conversation" with you in one of my other books.

Brett Thomas

OTHER BOOKS BY BRETT THOMAS

Integral Leadership: The World's First Unifying Theory of Leadership That Will Forever Transform How You Understand, Practice and Develop Leadership

Leadership Styles: How the Most Successful Leaders Adapt and Optimize Their Leadership Style to Maximize Their Influence and Impact.

Strategy & Alignment: How the Most Successful Leaders Analyze Needs, Find Leverage, Craft Vision, Align Stakeholders and Create Smart, Strategic Plans

Teamwork & Culture: How the Most Successful Leaders Create the Container, Communicate Effectively, and Consistently Keep Everyone Engaged and Motivated

Execution & Performance: How the Most Successful Leaders Close Expectation Gaps, Maintain High Accountability and Productivity, and Reliably Deliver Excellent Results

Blowing the Whistle on Bogus Leadership: Veteran Industry Insider Reveals Why the Leadership Development Industry is Not Developing Leaders.

The Leadership Rosetta Stone: Discover Which Leadership Approaches Will Work With Which People and Circumstances and Which Approaches Will Be Disastrous Failures with Which People and Circumstances

Accelerating Leadership: The Groundbreaking Method for Rapid Leadership Skill Development That Achieves Twice the Results in Half the Time at a Fraction of the Cost

Reinventing Leadership: Discover the Revolutionary Method That Thousands of Leaders and Organizations Are Using to Rapidly Improve Leadership Performance and Organizational Results

Worldviews: The Four Mindsets That Determine What People Perceive, Believe and Value, and Which Leadership Styles They Will Follow

Leadership Intelligence: Learn How Your Cognitive, Emotional, Social and Moral Development is Impacting Your Leadership Performance and How Leaders Can Now Benchmark and Boost These Intelligences

Handbook of Leadership Development: The Definitive Guide for Executives in Charge of Leadership Development

Leadership Psychology: How to Apply Crucial Insights from Positive Psychology, Developmental Psychology, Integral Psychology and Organizational Psychology to Develop More Effective Leaders (To be published in 2025)

ABOUT THE AUTHOR

Leadership authority Brett Thomas is an expert on leadership development, integral theory, and developmental psychology. He has written 14 books on management and leadership. In collaboration with Ken Wilber, he created the world's first "unifying theory of leadership" and wove together 100 years of leadership theory into a unified model that explains which theories and approaches will work with which people and circumstances that also accurately predicts which leadership styles and approaches will be disastrous failures with which specific types of people and circumstances. He is the creator (along with his mentor Ken Wilber) of the popular practice known as Integral Leadership. Brett's fourteen books are used as textbooks around the world in many of the top leadership training and coaching programs. Numerous institutions and academies teach various versions of Brett's highly respected Integral Leadership Program, sometimes using other names such as the Executive Leadership Program, the C-Suite Leadership Program, and the Integral Leadership MBA. Brett is a serial entrepreneur and leader working behind the scenes in more than a dozen humanitarian efforts under the umbrella of the international non-profit (501c3) he quietly founded years ago. Brett is the mentor, advisor, and coach to hundreds of CEOs. Dozens of his clients have scaled their companies from tens of millions to hundreds of millions in revenue and even to over a billion in some cases (while going from dozens to hundreds to thousands of employees), always with a "balanced scorecard" and "triple bottom line," meaning a rich, healthy, beloved culture never merely profit-seeking. In addition to writing books, Brett serves as an advisor to dozens of CEOs and C-Suite Executive Teams, serves as a fractional COO to several organizations, and teaches in several academies. In addition to co-founding two of the most respected and admired leadership academies in the world, he is also one of the primary co-founders of the Conscious Capitalism movement, which he helped launch nearly two decades ago to make "business a force for good."

www.ingramcontent.com/pod-product-compliance
Lightning Source LLC
Chambersburg PA
CBHW071051240526
45471CB00015B/1623